Int - Relations

BEING IN THE MIDDLE BY BEING
AT THE EDGE

D1328631

Cover Design by Lucy Evans

Dedicated to Ubima p'Udongi,
whose concern for truth
and for powerless people
caused him to become an intermediary
and cost him his life.
Killed in Pakwach, Uganda; July, 1992.

Being in the Middle by Being at the Edge

Quaker Experience of Non-official Political Mediation

by
Steven and Sue Williams

Quaker Peace & Service, London
in association with
Sessions Book Trust, York, England

ISBN 1 85072 139 4

Printed in 9¾ on 10¾ point Bembo Typeface from Author's Disk
by William Sessions Limited
The Ebor Press, York, England

Table of Contents

Preface

Quakers and political mediation

The Religious Society of Friends (Quakers)[1] is a very small denomination, probably nowhere claiming as much as 1% of the population. There are several Quakers known for having acted as mediators. Still, in the greater picture of world events, Quaker activities in political mediation play a very small role. Most violent international conflicts are finally settled by some combination of grass-roots work to change the setting and the possibilities, and high-profile negotiations or pressure to induce the major actors to agree to changes. Quakers have only ever had a very small part in this, working behind the scenes to help make it all possible. In an area of work also undertaken by the United Nations, by regional groupings of nations or large nations individually, by the World Council of Churches, and by the Vatican, to name but a few, the impact of Quakers is necessarily very humble.

Nonetheless, it seems to us that the Quaker role is distinctive, and little-known. For these reasons, we have set about to record something of our own and others' experience, trying to tease out some of the aspects distinctive to the "peculiar people called Quakers."

Intended audience

This is an attempt to collect and analyse some of the experiences of Quakers and Quaker representatives in the mediation of political conflict. We hope that it will be useful to those Friends and others who have acted as mediators, and to anyone who may take on this kind of role in future. We would particularly hope that people active in other kinds of mediation (family, neighbourhood, school, or whatever) would see these experiences as encouragement to consider that they, too, could act in the political arena, if needed.

Quakers are not the only audience aimed at. **IF YOU ARE NOT A QUAKER**, you may need to be patient with special words or concepts, and you may want to start with chapter 2 and come back to chapter 1 later, but we hope you will feel that this is for you, too. Although not exclusively aimed at Quakers, this record is based firmly on Quaker work, done by members of a religious body, for spiritual reasons, and we are not ashamed to call it a Quaker book.

The organisations which have supported this kind of work, notably Quaker Peace & Service (QPS) and the American Friends Service Committee (AFSC), are at the same time the source of much of what follows, and part of its intended audience. It also seems important to make these experiences available to the wider Society of Friends, in whose name the work is done, so that more of its members can provide guidance, testing, and support, as well as a pool of potential Quaker mediators.

In the belief that case studies provide the best learning, we will quote many stories and anecdotes to give the flavour of mediation and mediators, rather than remaining at an analytical distance.

Experience

This writing has grown out of our own experiences in political mediation under the auspices of Quaker Peace & Service, a department of London and Ireland[2] Yearly Meetings of the Religious Society of Friends, including four years as representatives in Northern Ireland and brief visits to Uganda. We have been able to travel during 1991-92 to consult Quakers and others doing work similar to ours, in other parts of the world. The persons consulted during this period are listed in Appendix II. The 1989 Old Jordans consultation on political mediation[3] also provided important insights and opportunities to share with colleagues.

The experiences described here are from a combination of sources. Many are our own. Rather than write in the first person (as we are doing in this preface), we have chosen to write in the third person, to make it clear that the observations and insights are not ours alone, but come from a number of other people who have generously given us their time and ideas. In telling our own anecdotes, we will follow the same format as for others — indenting each anecdote or quotation, with a footnote at the bottom.

Many of the quotations are taken from transcripts of conversations we have had with other Quaker mediators. These were done with the understanding that we would quote only agreed sections of the conversations. Much of the detail of these discussions was off-the-record, but has served as background for some of the unattributed statements in the text.

A note about style and terminology

Our own experience has been in Northern Ireland and Uganda, with a variety of people who might be described as politicians, government ministers, civil servants, army commanders, paramilitaries, rebels, bandits, dissidents, militants, terrorists, diplomats, advisors, city officials, party functionaries, and others. In other situations, any of these people might be referred to with a variety of other words. We have chosen to try to limit the terms, for the sake of clarity, but with the understanding that this is an abstraction from reality. In using terms like "politician" or "political leader," we mean to refer to people in elected or appointed public positions, or affiliated to main-stream political parties. The terms "armed group" or "paramilitary" will refer to people who belong to groupings, often illegal, which are engaged in violent acts in opposition to the existing government. This is not to suggest that governments do not use violence. Nor is it to deny that the relative positions might change tomorrow: as everyone knows, today's terrorist is tomorrow's freedom-fighter and founder of the state. This use of terms is simply to try to describe a different set of actors, one in possession of the legal right to use weapons, the other resorting to weapons without the sanction of law and power. Whether there are additional distinctions — whether, for example, one group is elected, another self-selected — varies too much according to the situation, to permit of a general rule.

For reasons of confidentiality, these people will not be named. Individual members or leaders of all of these groupings will generally be **referred to as politicians, and as "he"**, in the third person singular. There are, of course, some women politicians, diplomats, and civil servants. There are relatively few female army commanders or paramilitaries in the situations we have dealt with. For the sake of clarity, to avoid constant repetitions of the same nouns and confusion of pronouns, we will generally use the terms politicians and he. Correspondingly, persons taking a third-party role in conflict will be called mediators, though many would not use that name for themselves, and **a mediator will be referred to as "she."** This is not because many are women; on the contrary, the vast majority of people engaged in political mediation are male. But it is, again, easier for the writers to write, and for readers to distinguish between characters, with this small convention. We do not think that we harbour a sub-conscious belief that women make better mediators or have characteristics that are more suitable for mediation, but it is difficult to guarantee that there is no such hidden agenda. We would emphasise, however, that this use of "he" and "she" is merely to distinguish the type of person being referred to - either politician or mediator - and does not necessarily correspond to the actual sex of the person.

Our own mediation has generally been done as a team of two, with another individual or two occasionally joining in. Some mediators work alone, some in teams. Where this difference is relevant, it will be explored in more detail. Otherwise, the singular will normally be employed for general statements about mediation.

Mediation efforts in perspective

Mediation takes place in a context in which much other work must be done, to change the cultures, to build new structures, to create a space where enemies can meet. The success of mediation and negotiation will depend greatly on this larger work of reconciliation. A continuing theme in this discussion will be the importance of valuing and supporting all these ways of working, rather than emphasising one to the exclusion of others. It may never be clear which approach, which activity, which structure gave the final push to bring about change, but this is not important. What is vital is to work together as well as possible, humbled by the efforts of others, but also encouraged.

What is described here is, ultimately, a very small section of a spectrum of activities that ranges from single meetings of lower-level figures to a full-blown gathering of government representatives to agree the formal ending of a war. The experience of Friends has generally been of long involvement at a variety of levels — perhaps most often in the middle of this spectrum. At the time of writing, there is more attention than in quite some time being devoted to the latter end of this spectrum, with the United Nations (UN), the European Community (EC), and private groups such as the Carter Center[4] all sending envoys to try to sort out violent conflicts in different parts of the world. The United States and the Commonwealth of Independent States are among the nations trying to push along the Middle East talks. There are periodic announcements of cease-fires in Bosnia-Herzegovina and Nagorno-Karabakh, talks in Rome between

Renamo and the government of Mozambique which led to a cease-fire agreement, delayed negotiations of the Conference for a Democratic South Africa, and the overseeing of discussions and agreements in Central America. These high-profile processes are dramatic and important. Behind and ahead lie years of work by others, toiling away in obscurity in a tapestry of beautifully different ways of working. Quaker mediation constitutes one fragment of that tapestry.

Definitions

A note about definitions of terms, such as mediation and facilitation, appears at the end in Appendix I.

Acknowledgement

We would like to acknowledge the support and encouragement of so many people during this period of travel, reflection, and writing over the past two years. The Joseph Rowntree Charitable Trust and the Barrow and Geraldine S. Cadbury Trust provided generous funding, advice, and questions, which made this time possible. Two Quaker study centres, Pendle Hill (Pennsylvania, USA) and Woodbrooke College (Birmingham, England), gave us congenial space and other assistance with writing. Quaker Peace & Service allowed us to continue to be "associates" at a distance.

Particularly we would like to thank Val Ferguson, Stephen Pittam, and Andrew Clark who helped us to envision and implement this project. Thanks again to Joseph Rowntree Charitable Trust for financing the publication of this book, to Bob Neidhardt and Daniel Silvey for their assistance with the publication arrangements, and to Val Ferguson and Steve Gove for checking the final proofs. Also, special thanks to all those we have consulted and interviewed, as well as to those who have read and commented on the various drafts of this writing.

Sue and Steve Williams
1994

CHAPTER 1

Quaker Principles, Concern and Collective Testing

WITHIN THE RELIGIOUS SOCIETY OF FRIENDS, the belief that the divine spirit may express itself through any individual leads to what is called "concern": the individual's profound, spiritually-based commitment to take on a particular piece of work. This might be a concern about the plight of a particular group of people who are suffering or in conflict or oppressed in some way. It might be a concern to do something about a particular social problem, such as alcoholism or homelessness. The Society respects this concern, sometimes authorises individuals to do this work on their behalf, and may even "release" individuals by providing for their subsistence needs while they live out this concern. The process requires, however, that the concern be tested by the group, in a searching of conscience and the divine will, against the principles and traditions of Friends, as well as in practical and other ways.

> Sometimes there may come a leading to some specific task, felt by [the individual] as an imperative claim of God upon him not to be denied even if he feels personal reluctance. This is what Friends call a concern, an experience they have known throughout their history.
>
> It has been the practice for a Friend, who believes that he has heard such a call, to bring the concern before the gathered community of Friends in his monthly meeting, that it may be tested as a true leading of the Spirit. The practice is an expression of our membership of one another, of a mutually accepted obligation, that of the individual Friend to test his concern against the counsel of the group, and that of the group to seek the guidance of God in exercising its judgment. It may bring enrichment both to the individual and to the group, even though the meeting may advise the Friend that he is mistaken. If he is encouraged to go forward, the prayers of Friends will strengthen him in his service.[5]

Mediation has often been done on the basis of individual concern. Many Quaker mediators have acted on the basis of spiritual motivation, but while engaged in other work. Others acted as representatives of Quaker organisations or bodies, often based on their personal concern about a situation. Still others were "released" or enabled to act in an individual capacity, but somehow connected with Friends. In all of these kinds of arrangements, there is a role for some group to be involved in guidance, supervision, and overseeing of the process, as well as testing the individual's motivation and supporting those engaged in the work. When individual Friends are acting as mediators, it is not always clear which "hat" they are wearing, and to whom they are accountable. Ultimately, of course, they are accountable to God; but, if they are identifying themselves as members of the Religious Society of Friends, then the larger body of Friends needs to be aware of their activities and to offer some collective guidance to the individual acting under concern.

Quaker beliefs and principles

The phrase most commonly used by Quaker mediators to explain their work is the belief in "that of God" in each individual they deal with. They respond to the spark of goodness at the heart of each person, and this permits them to deal on equal terms with people on various sides of a dispute. This belief leads the Quaker mediator to approach relationships with all sides in a spirit of love and tolerance that can be quite disarming. Adam Curle refers to a kind of "realization that makes it possible for us to relate deeply, at the level of shared Ground of being, with all human beings." Continuing, he says:

> To the extent that we ourselves are open to the divine truth within ourselves, we try to share it with all we encounter. I don't mean by proselytizing, of course, but by recognising and loving their essential holiness and thereby liberating them, to some extent, from horrifying compulsions of fear and hatred, and hence, violence.[6]

As there is good in each person, so there is truth in each, and validity in each one's experiences, however different from the experiences of the "other side". Rather than choose sides, mediators try to bring the different sides together, not only by arranging direct meetings, but by helping each to understand the other's actions and statements, and by encouraging everyone to think and behave more humanely and creatively. In order to do this, they must build their own relationships with people on each side, learning about their experiences, feelings, and hopes, as well as their political views.

Individual mediators operate out of a commitment to respect all sides, but this does not mean that they are immune to the pain of each situation. The individual's conscience also pushes for caring for victims, alleviation of suffering, and taking a stand against injustice. In these conflicts, there is usually violence and often injustice, and one or the other of these may be disproportionately on one side. If the power imbalance is great enough, the situation may not be an appropriate one for mediation. H W van der Merwe describes a situation in which he, and the Centre for Intergroup Studies which he directed, attempted to intervene as an impartial third party between the black community and the white authorities at a time of widespread disturbances in Cape Town, South Africa, in 1976.

A spontaneous shift in the role of the Centre developed as it became more involved in the issues of the local situation characterized by asymmetry of power and social injustice. This shift was due to several factors and was evident in several actions:

1. The need to assist the black community in their negotiations, in their pleas for protection against police as well as hooligans [...] drew the Centre towards the protesting party in the conflict. [...]

2. [...] The consultations called by the Centre which were, from the beginning, poorly attended by government spokesmen. [...]

3. The fact that the Centre submitted evidence almost exclusively concerned with the injustices of the present apartheid policy, the failure of white officials and alleged police brutality and intimidation, inevitably caused tension with the establishment and more specifically the police. [...] This situation was further aggravated when the director [H W van der Merwe] felt compelled to refute statements about the local political and economic situation made by senior police officers while giving evidence.[7]

In this case, the shift from mediation to advocacy was done with openness, and as part of a life committed to facilitating communication between the opponents, so that H W was able afterward to continue as an intermediary with the respect and trust of both sides. But the tension is common to mediators, as different truths and different beliefs must be balanced in each action.

Collective testing

Most Quaker mediators feel that they are trusted, not only as individuals, but because they are connected to the larger corporate body of Friends. The individual is, in some sense, living out a caring and a commitment shared by the group. The group is testing the general train of activities, setting policy and priorities, lending its ideas and good sense. This collective involvement is both a support and a discipline. Some mediators feel a lack of the support from the group; others chafe under the constraint of the group's discipline; but most are committed to this part of the process, even while working to improve it. And, although many of the political figures involved in Quaker conferences or mediation may not know the precise process of collective testing, they do presume that the individuals they are dealing with represent a larger group of concerned people, who exercise some guidance or oversight over what happens, and whose commitment in time and resources is greater than an individual would provide.

In order for this collective testing to be effective, several things are needed. The individual representative or mediator must accept guidance. The group offering guidance must have appropriate skills and experience. All involved must accept that they seek, not to get their own way, but to discern what is right, what is the divine will, in the situation that confronts them. In this respect, while the mediator is expected to develop a high degree of expertise and professionalism in doing the work, the starting point for everyone involved is spiritual qualities, and the corporate testing depends on discernment as much as on expertise.

Most often, the collective guidance is provided by a committee. During the India-Pakistan war of 1965, for example, the Friends Service Council in London created an India-Pakistan Advisory Group, while on the other side of the Atlantic the American Friends Service Committee established the Pakistan-India Advisory Group. Together, these two groups provided guidance for the Quaker initiative in the region during the next several years. Mike Yarrow describes the early role of the committees:

> Before the second meeting of the Pakistan-India Advisory Group in Washington, December 21, 1965, arrangements and schedules had been roughed out for a team visit starting in mid-January. The group supplied the team members, two of whom were present at the meeting, with many suggestions on procedure and substantive issues, but avoided restrictive instructions. Prominent in the deliberations was the plan of moving back and forth between the two countries with the aim of strengthening the moderates on both sides who might work toward a solution. The team was asked to work closely with the resident Quaker staff in the two countries and to bring back recommendations for ongoing work in the future.[8]

This structure offered special opportunities for advice, and possible stumbling-blocks as well, since it involved two distant and administratively different Quaker bodies in supervising the mediation team. In the event, both the visiting team and their dual committees seem to have worked well together.[9] The visiting team formed their day-to-day programme on the basis suggested by the committee, in the light of events and their own increasing understanding of the situation and its possibilities.

Ideally, committees guiding mediation develop over time a profound understanding of the conflict situation, the possibilities for peace-making, and the role of its representatives. As the work develops, the experiences and activities of the representatives may take most of the committee's attention, but this must be seen against the backdrop of the group commitment and the group discernment. "The experience has got to be shared in such a way that the general spiritual commitment can be regularly brought back down for a reality test."[10] The committee has a special responsibility to keep in mind the basic principles on which the work was begun, and to keep pointing out, supporting, and challenging aspects of the programme as they relate to the deeper and more profound issues. In this sense, the committee members need not be more expert in regional issues than the field staff; instead, their value is in bringing to bear other questions, basic priorities, and longer time-frames.

Possible problems with committees

This process of collective testing can present difficulties, however, if it endangers confidentiality or balance. When there are issues of great moment at a delicate point in their development, or when people are communicating privately before their contact can be made public, information must be shared among as few people as possible. For this reason, as Trevor Jepson reports, the Southern Africa Working Group did not refer publicly to its initiative in Rhodesia/Zimbabwe.

Anyone searching the minutes for information on how decisions were reached on direct involvement in mediation would be disappointed. The first reference to a Quaker presence at the Rhodesia Conference in Geneva in 1976 was curiously oblique: it was simply to record that another Friend had to chair a meeting of the Working Group because its regular chairman was in Geneva! The intensive series of visits to southern Africa by Friends during 1978 and 1979 received no mention.

It would have been necessary for Walter Martin, then General Secretary of Friends Service Council, to secure support of the Council, through its Chairman, for the initiatives he was wanting to undertake, but this would have been by word of mouth and shared with a fairly small circle. [...] Whether this level of confidentiality was strictly necessary is an interesting question, but it did not imply a lack of accountability. Careful notes were made following (not during) all meetings and conversations with the parties, usually brought back personally by the people making them, and would have been seen by the same small group of Friends.[11]

This was not because anyone actually feared there might be a spy on the committee, but simply in order to limit the possible sources of unintentional leaks, while providing careful oversight by a small group.

Most committees can be counted on to be entirely scrupulous about confidentiality, but sometimes the members' own priorities may conflict with the needs of the mediation process.

When you have a committee which is knowledgeable and sympathetic with the nature of the experience that's going on, we could come back from one of our seminars where we'd brought together some Israelis and some Palestinians, not in a secret meeting, because we never had secret meetings. It might be a confidential one, totally off the record. We'd report that, of course, at a meeting like this we can't identify all the participants... If any of you want to know, come and talk, but it won't be in the written minutes. And, as we give our report now, we won't attribute positions to people, but we'll state some of the broad areas that came out. A committee who has worked on the Middle East will smile and listen carefully, and then they'll ask some interesting questions, but will stay away from pressing us, because they know that, if that were to become public, you've lost it all.

There's a strain, and that is, every now and then, people who define a form of peace education in the United States have reached a point where they don't have a depth of respect for the parties involved, and they have a shorter term political horizon and political agenda. And they get very discomforted with not only this kind of activity, but also the fact that you haven't yet come up with some other clear definition they want.[12]

Other organisational priorities, then, may interfere with the discernment that needs to be brought to bear on this area of work. The tensions are important ones, healthy ones, because Friends need to do peace education and other work as well as mediation. But the collective guidance offered should not be the criticism of one kind of work for not being another, but the careful, corporate attempt to see what ought to happen, what would be the divine will, in this particular situation. For this reason, committees or groups selected in order to provide testing and guidance may best be generalists, or specialists in common sense and faith in practice, rather than experts "representing" other disciplines or areas of work. This is not to suggest that decisions should be taken out of ignorance about the issues and problems in the conflict situation. But the knowledge that members bring to a committee must be blended with their depth of concern and experience, so that they might identify in this situation the "ways that seem to be opening" - as Quakers say - whether these ways are reconciliation or confrontation, relief or development.

One of the dangers of this commitment to corporate testing is that the opportunity for intervening in a helpful way could pass before Friends are able to come to complete unity on the way forward. No matter how long a committee may labour over a decision of whether to get involved in a particular conflict, there may still be doubts and reservations within the group. If there is some urgency in the situation, as of course there usually is when people are engaged in violent conflict and people are being killed every day, it may be necessary and appropriate for the committee to nominate or appoint some representatives to test the concern by going to where the conflict is happening and spending some time with people on each side. Out of this direct engagement in the situation, the representatives may be able to find more clarity about a role for Quakers. This is a "reality test" that can make a spiritual concern relevant and appropriate to the people who are living with the conflict on a daily basis. It is nearly impossible to test a concern if one is not engaged in some way with the area of concern. Yet it has to be kept in mind that concern may require the individuals and the organisation to make a long-term commitment.

> It must not be thought that a Quaker mediating role can be switched on and off at will. It requires real concern, which should lead to deep commitment, perhaps for a period extending over many years.[13]

So the individual concern must be tested corporately, but the corporate decision-making process must be guided by the reality of the situation as seen through the eyes of individuals on the spot. And this entire process should be grounded in spiritual direction and faith. The testing then leads to some action, unless it is decided that the concern is not one that the Society of Friends can support and sustain. If action is taken — an action that Quakers will support — it may often be a different action than what was originally suggested by the individual under concern. Support, in this context, means spiritual support in prayer and worship, financial support through contributions, and personal support by Friends coming forward to undertake the work that is envisioned. In all these ways, the individual and the collective commitment dove-tail in the living out of faith in action.

6

CHAPTER 2

Establishing Credibility

QUAKERS ARE A SMALL GROUP, with no particular power or influence in the world. Why would parties in conflict trust them to act as intermediaries? The reasons may have to do with the history or past activities of Quakers as a group, or with something about the individual that creates trust.

Reputation

Quakers have, over the years, been active in various types of relief and assistance in times of war and violence. This has given the Society of Friends the reputation of a religious group that is willing to help victims on all sides of a conflict.

Quaker representatives in many places have been told how Friends had assisted people in a way that was remembered positively. Irish Friends are known for having assisted people during the famine of the 1840's without regard for their politics or religious affiliation. More recently, in the early 1970's, Quakers took in families who were burned out of their houses in West Belfast, and assisted families of people from both sides of the political divide who were interned and imprisoned. In Germany, Quakers are remembered for their relief and child-feeding programmes after the two World Wars.

This reputation is important, because it is based on solid, local experience. It does not guarantee that a newly-arrived Quaker can be trusted with regard to analysis or confidentiality, but it does show that the Society of Friends is concerned to try to relieve suffering on any side, and that is a good foundation. Clarence Pickett, writing about Quaker service in Europe during 1938-39, says:

> In the total European tragedy of many millions uprooted and persecuted, the service which our European workers could render was indeed relatively small. Yet in proportion to the size of the staffs, it was surprisingly large, because we had been in those countries a long time, were trusted as having no purpose except to be of help, and also our international contacts and channels were the result of more than twenty years' consistent work. It would be hard to exaggerate the advantage of this kind of long-time contact in such an hour of crisis. A worker finds he can call on a wide variety of strong and useful persons and organisations, not through any virtue of his own, but because of what those who have preceded him have built up in the way of confidence. This is an

7

experience which in turn gives one a sense of the greatest possible responsibility to his on-going organisation.[14]

Sometimes there is a very specific contact made through a Quaker project that later turns out to be crucial for the credibility of Quakers as mediators. Elmore Jackson, who undertook a mediation mission between Israel and Egypt in 1955, tells of the importance of contacts made during Quaker administration of a UN-sponsored refugee relief programme in Gaza in 1949:

> During the early weeks of the Gaza operation a unit of about three thousand Egyptian troops remained encircled by Israeli forces at Faluja in the Negev, not far from the Gaza Strip. Gamal Abdel Nasser, then a colonel in the Egyptian army, was serving as Chief of Staff to Said Taha, an Egyptian brigade commander in the enclave. With the encouragement of the United Nations, Quakers negotiated agreements with the Israelis and with the Egyptian army that permitted food supplies to be taken through the Israeli and Egyptian lines to the local civilian population in the enclave, which, like the Egyptian forces, were cut off from all outside sources of food supply. Colonel Nasser handled the negotiations on behalf of the Egyptian army and carried out the subsequent distribution to the complete satisfaction of the Quaker group. [...] A relationship of confidence developed that led to several long evenings in which Colonel Nasser and the Quaker convoy team sat around darkening campfires discussing differences and similarities between Quaker and Islamic thought. [...] It was the Gaza relief operation - and especially the relationship of confidence that developed with Nasser at Faluja - which set the stage for the Egyptian approach to Quakers in the spring of 1955.[15]

Friends beginning work in the Middle East inherit a particularly vast tapestry of previous Quaker work and contacts, from attempts to safeguard Jews and others at risk from the Holocaust, to assistance to Jewish refugees and later to Palestinian refugees, to contemporary work with human rights organisations, peace groups, and kindergartens.

There are also people in the region who know Quakers from our work in the past. Many Israelis remember the work of Quakers in Europe before and during the second World War assisting Jewish refugees. Unfortunately, other Israelis do not remember this, but rather remember the Quaker position articulated in the AFSC book Search for Peace in the Middle East, which they consider to be partisan. (I consider it to be rather nonpartisan and pragmatic.) Changing that impression is one challenge we have faced. We also encounter alumni of Quaker conferences held elsewhere — New York, Geneva, even Tokyo.[16]

Quaker work with diplomats at the United Nations as well as Quaker conferences programmes over the years have been important points of contact for a generation

8

of young diplomats, many of whom are now in positions of considerable authority and influence in their own countries. The Geneva Friends Centre at the headquarters of the League of Nations was opened in September 1922, and in 1949 was reactivated as a second point of Quaker contact with the United Nations - the first being Quaker House in New York, established in 1948 in order "to reach persons who could influence trends toward war and peace."[17] Quaker conferences for diplomats began in 1952 with a gathering in Clarens, Switzerland, and these continued for many years. This pattern of conferences was extended to South Asia in 1955 and to Japan in 1965. Many of the participants "have reached positions of distinction in the diplomatic field" and remember the experience of these conferences very positively.[18] A Quaker who is involved with the situation in Sri Lanka describes his experience when he first visited refugees from one of the "sides" there:

> I met many people, some of whom had been to Quaker conferences. They said: "You don't have to tell us anything about the Quakers, we know about you. If you people are interested in peace, don't waste your time, come soon."[19]

Friends' involvement in education has also had a positive impact in some situations. For example, the Friends' School in Ramallah (West Bank) has educated a number of people who are now leading personalities in the Palestinian community, and the Quaker representatives in the Middle East have credibility with these people because of their educational experiences.

> Friends education has been very important in the region, very important. But there's not a multiplier effect on that. People who have been educated in Quaker institutions you almost immediately have a rapport with. But in terms of that person's experience being multiplied in Arab society, no.[20]

So credibility in situations of conflict depends, to some extent, on previous activities that are perceived to be balanced in providing assistance to all sides. This credibility arises from the personal contacts and experiences that people have had with Quakers in the past and, in some cases, may be passed down through generations. In other cases, Quakers have credibility with the individual contacts, but there is no "multiplier effect". Sometimes, previous experience with Quaker programmes can leave people with a negative view of Quakers:

> We were in Uganda for three months during 1991, as a result of a request that had come to QPS from Ugandans who were trying to mediate in a particular conflict there. While visiting the region of conflict, we happened to meet a staff member from the British High Commission who was there to assess the security situation. He was surprised to find Quakers there. We had a general discussion about the situation in that region and how his government might assist. At the end of the conversation, he admitted to us that he did not have

9

a very positive view of Quakers. Some years before, when he had been involved with East-West work in the Foreign Office in London, he had attended a session of the London Diplomats' Group of Quaker Peace & Service. The speaker at this session was a Soviet diplomat, who he felt had just given them "the party line." His view of Quakers at the time was that they were just giving this person a platform to spread his propaganda and that there was nothing new or interesting in what had been said. He did not, therefore, ever attend another Quaker diplomats' group.[21]

So, previous contact with Friends may be either positive or negative for the particular individuals that Quaker mediators might meet, and, in regions where there has been a great deal of previous contact, the mixture of impressions may be quite complex. Without exception, the Quaker representatives consulted by the authors felt that they gained enormously from work done and reputations established by other Friends, and they acknowledged a sense of gratitude and humility at becoming heirs to this predisposition to trust them.

Individuals' credibility

Ultimately, credibility has to be established by the individuals who are trying to put themselves in the mediating role. Many of the key people in a particular conflict may never have met a Quaker before, and may never have considered having a third person help with communication or meetings. Sometimes, an introduction or recommendation from someone they do know and trust can be helpful. Or, the potential mediator may have some personal involvement in the situation which demonstrates a commitment to or a concern for the particular country or region that is in conflict.

Simon Fisher, when he and his wife Jane were representatives of Quaker Peace & Service in Southern Africa, was asked to visit a particular refugee camp to inspect the conditions there.

I saw signs that the refugees had been tortured in their home country, and heard reports that it was at the hands of a particular brigade. The refugees asked me to see their government, tell them of this evidence, but also say that the refugees wanted to go home. Would the government guarantee their safety if they returned?

I saw the president and a minister. As it happened, I had got to know them, years before, when working as a teacher. And we and other Quakers had tried to help the minister when he was in prison during the colonial regime.

They were willing to listen, and I felt that they believed what I said. I later heard, through other sources, that my message had come at a good moment, when the government was trying to decide how to proceed on this issue.[22]

On many occasions, mediators have been able to act because they already knew key figures, had proven themselves in some way, and were able to re-activate a good relationship. These old links cannot be built on demand; the moment they are needed is too late to establish them. But they can be very useful.

10

It may be important that the Quakers are seen to be involved in a variety of ways, not just coming in from outside wanting to mediate. One of the Quaker staff at the UN has described it this way:

I think it's in those processes where you're not there with your "I'm a mediator" flag, but where you're there as part of a Quaker team, that you establish the relationships which then make people willing to explore the relationship further.... I think it's very difficult to set up a store with a sign over it saying: MEDIATION. Mediation comes, almost always, on the basis of relationships that are already established, or that are going to be established, not self-consciously, [as] if you had a little boutique that said: MEDIATION, people would stop in when they need it.[23]

So there is a need for the mediator to become known to the parties in conflict in a natural way, but in a way that would lead them to believe that this person can be trusted. It involves a kind of being known that makes one's presence unremarkable and accepted by all the parties. This is the credibility that comes from a longer-term commitment to a particular situation and a particular set of people.

The most obvious thing is that people come to know you. You walk into a room, and there's not the whole ritual of having to get to know who you are, to feel each other out. You gain the sense over time that you can begin a conversation in the middle. You can begin where you left off a while ago. And that's not trivial. When you're dealing with a situation which is in flux, you don't have to go through the total sounding-out again each time. And that does make a difference. I think the other thing that occurs is one of, for lack of a better word, trust. And I mean it in the least strong sense, that is, they roughly know who you are, and know roughly what to expect, and, if you've gotten along well, you're at a plateau. So there isn't a lot of hiding of views.[24]

Establishing one's credibility can be a delicate task. It is necessary to indicate that one has useful contacts, and could be trusted with confidential messages, without appearing to be overly anxious to "sell" oneself.

There is a tension between the need for privacy and the need for going public. [...] I was very conscious of this the other night at a party. A man from the Telegraph, a senior journalist, knows South Africa a lot, but he didn't know my name. He asked me what I was doing, and I told him. Then he said: "I'm sure you're not exaggerating," which means that he does think I'm exaggerating. Then I thought it was time for me to shut up.[25]

Anything resembling the approach of a salesman will be counter-productive, because having to trumpet one's own mediation skill or analytical ability may simply convince political figures that these are lacking. These are qualities that will need to be

11

demonstrated and tested over time. It may, however, occasionally be necessary to assure the parties of one's discretion and one's contacts on the other sides, understanding that these will also need to be tested. As mediators, Quakers generally seem to try to be accurate and humble at the same time, perhaps erring in the direction of modesty.

Status

Some Friends who have acted as mediators have felt that their credibility came, in part, from other sources of status: being academics or lawyers, or being associated with a particular institution or international body. Age and demeanour may also be important initial sources of credibility, particularly in societies where grey hairs connote experience and wisdom. In the case of a team of mediators, having a range of nationalities, professions, and international experiences can give great weight. Mediators have also sometimes been introduced by local people of stature, and a bit of credibility has rubbed off accordingly. All of this is, of course, only the immediate, surface sort of credibility that gives access to someone for one meeting. After that, other factors will be evaluated.

Aspects of credibility

In addition to being known, the mediator must demonstrate a genuine willingness to listen to the points of view of all the parties involved. Often the question of who else the mediator knows will be an issue for building credibility. If the politician wants to know something about the views of another side, then the mediator's credibility will depend upon being able to demonstrate first-hand contact with significant people on that other side. Likewise, if a political figure wants to be able to communicate with that other side through a third party, then credibility will depend on the mediator's ability to get prompt access to key people on the other side and to convey messages and responses accurately.

In a general conversation with the leader of a political party, I mentioned that I would be travelling the next day to another city, and meeting with politicians there. Was there anything in particular he would like me to convey to them? He got up, closed the door, lowered his voice, and asked: "How close can you get to the leader there?" I said I thought I could get quite close. He proceeded to state and re-state a message, which I delivered; and I brought back a response. The first chap smiled thinly and said he had tried repeatedly to send this message through another channel, but without success.

This was the beginning of a long and active relationship. Although he was generally regarded as unapproachable and uninterested in any contact with the other side, he used us as intermediaries in a number of ways. And he commented pointedly, on several occasions, that he had never seen or heard any other reference to any of the contacts we were involved in on his behalf. This was particularly noticeable, as he had ended abruptly his relationship with a more prominent intermediary who had publicly claimed credit for his role.[26]

12

Another aspect of credibility, then, is the testing of the confidentiality of the relationship. Once past the initial stage, where previous contact with Quakers or quick sources of status may matter, the credibility of the mediator will be part of the whole relationship. The problem will move from establishing credibility to extending it or maintaining it, in the context of relationships. In this process, as is clear in the preceding anecdote, trustworthiness and discretion seem to become more important than visibility. For those in the position of Quakers, without power, influence, or funding to offer, the ability to remain unseen and work without kudos is an important asset.

CHAPTER 3

Being in the Middle: Neutrality?
Impartiality?

IN A WONDERFUL, BRIEF SUMMARY of a complex dilemma, Khalil Mahshi, headmaster
of Friends Schools, Ramallah, said:

> Remaining in the middle means being at the edge in terms of what you believe
> in.[27]

The decision to stay in the middle, as mediators do, is not to stay on the fence. On the
contrary, it means a constant testing of one's own beliefs and actions, and the awareness
of occupying a very marginal position at the fringe of a society in conflict.

The dynamics of conflict push people to choose sides and stay there, even more
than in ordinary society. Loyalty is a key quality, and is often expressed by holding to
the choices made and sides upheld by parents and grandparents. It is difficult for people
in such a situation to believe that anyone can listen to more than one view, can understand conflicting sets of feelings and experiences, can sympathise with more than one
side. This disbelief must be confronted and overcome by the mediator, at an early stage
in the work. But it can only be overcome by long, patient work: by listening again and
again to the "party line" until it is possible to move on, by the repeated willingness to
try to convey to other people various views one may not share, and simply by being
around and coming back to each person regardless of what one hears elsewhere or what
happens in the unfolding of the conflict.

Trusted to be fair

Clearly, one of the prerequisites for mediators is that they be trusted. This can
be defined either negatively or positively: that they be trusted not to favour one side
over another, or that they be trusted to understand each side sympathetically. Often,
attention is focused on meeting the negative criterion at the expense of the positive;
indeed, in polarised situations, the problem may most often be expressed and thought
of in negative, suspicious terms. In Northern Ireland, the search for a neutral chairperson for talks ran into problems, with numerous possible candidates being rejected by one
side or another. The assumption was that anyone who had ever met any of the

14

participants or said anything about the situation was inevitably partisan. This stalemate finally produced the suggestion that the ideal candidate would speak no English and know nothing about the situation: this, it was presumed, would guarantee impartiality.

Most Quaker mediators, on the contrary, stress the positive definition. Ignorance is not an appropriate basis for this role. What is needed, instead, is what has sometimes been called "balanced partiality",[28] that is, being concerned about and attached to all sides rather than none. This requires a new way of thinking about partiality. Rather than defining sympathy or attachment by whom it excludes, it is necessary to live out the belief that one can care about each side and each individual without shifting the balance unfairly in their direction.

The experience of politicians is that people either agree with them on all major issues, or disagree with them on all, and those who disagree, do so immediately and vehemently. They are sometimes initially uncomfortable with someone who listens, asks questions, and seems to want to understand, without expressing either agreement or disagreement. Is this non-committal person judging me without speaking? Disagreeing without being brave enough to say so? Secretly agreeing, but trying to pretend to be neutral? Quaker mediators often have the great advantage at this stage of being accepted as pacifists, and therefore able to disagree with the politician without being suspected of wanting to kill him. Only over time, and as the relationship grows, does the political or paramilitary leader begin to go beyond tolerating this strange behaviour, and perhaps begin to see it as useful. But it is an important stage, if one expects opponents at war with each other to sit down and talk together.

A bridge crosses over to the other side

Mediators work in polarised situations, in which the various sides create boundaries and walls to keep from knowing each other. Even within each side, there will be factions proclaiming that they are the only true voice, and insisting that others are not worth bothering with.

Mediators need to balance their contacts with a variety of people. In polarised situations, politicians may add to their value by refusing contact with any side. Those who are more elusive require more work by the mediator to build a relationship and to agree to meet with others, but give the mediator and the process more credibility if they participate.

There are some, perhaps "moderates", who are willing to talk - to the mediators, and to opponents. This makes them useful allies, but not so sought-after by others, and sometimes dismissed as irrelevant.

At the fringes are the political actors who won't talk, or whom others will not talk with. These may include the extremists, the armed groups, those who don't altogether trust talking, in any case. But these extremists will have to be drawn into the process eventually, if reconciliation and peace are to be brought about. And they will remember who met with them when they were pariahs, when the common wisdom was that to meet with them would only lend them a credibility they did not deserve. The mediator seems to have an obligation to balance [her] efforts, facilitating and supporting those who will talk, encouraging those who might talk someday, and keeping contact with those at the edges whom no one wants to talk to.[29]

There is often pressure on the mediator to demonstrate sympathy and understanding by refusing to hear certain sides of an issue or refusing to deal with certain people. In this sense also, the mediation process requires a shift in thinking, and it must be emphasised from the beginning. The mediator is useful primarily as a channel between those who have no direct contact. However agonising the conflict and the suffering, it will only finally be stopped when the different sides are able to work out an agreement. So the mediator must be clear from the beginning that this is the intention, that this is inherent in the role and in the process. Even if people are not yet ready for direct contact, or do not want public acknowledgement of any indirect contact, the break will have to be bridged if the situation is ever to change.

When I started the facilitation in Natal, I had a young student, as a research assistant, and he went ahead of me there to collect information. So I came there and we discussed our programme for the next day, and then he said that his biggest problem is that, if he goes to see the UDF, and the Inkatha people see him going there, how can he hide it from them. So I said: "No, your job is to make it known to Inkatha that you visit them [UDF], otherwise you're no use to them." It's still a problem with my young staff. They think that we should be cautious so that we don't get contaminated with the conservative people, and this is a very natural thing because we are inclined in that direction. So this is something that you have to inculcate and encourage, that you have to be seen on both sides.[30]

As H W says, it is a "very natural thing" to be attached to one side or repelled by another side. But it is possible for one to become attached to more than one side and to help the parties on each side to recognise the usefulness of having someone they can trust who has these attachments to all sides. People who are deeply engaged in conflict, particularly the leaders, are often the first to recognise their need to know and understand their opponents. The mediator offers them the opportunity to do this in an indirect and confidential way that will not compromise their position with their own side. But the mediator must also be looking for the right time and opportunity for the opponents to meet directly, to experience directly the sharing of experiences and the building of a shared reality.

Listening

A commitment to maintain a balance, even a balanced partiality, is not a mainstream belief, and requires actions which are not usual. The mediator must discipline herself to be able to listen to a very wide range of views and experiences. And more than just listening, she must listen sympathetically to each of the sides.

Somebody asked us in South Africa when we were doing a seminar: "Well, what happens when you find that you just can't listen sympathetically to one side any more?" And we said: "That's a clear indication to us that we haven't been listening to their experience recently. We've been listening to their party positions, but we haven't been listening to the human experience." And that means we need to go back and do that again. We need to go back to somebody on that side and say: "Tell us how you ended up in this position." Then we will hear again the story that will make it humanly possible to empathise with that person. You never get that by listening to party positions.[31]

So the mediator listens to the experience and begins to understand experiences and the human side of the individuals in conflict. This is the side of a person that is not acknowledged nor recognised by his opponents. It is often the point at which the mediator can help the enemies begin to see some common ground between themselves. Experiences they share might include the loss of a family member or a close friend in the conflict. There may be personal experiences of discrimination or persecution by people from the other side that have led to fear, anger, and hatred. Some may have had to choose between entering politics or taking up arms against the opponent.

All of these are experiences that the mediator may hear on each side. There will come a point in her relationship with each side when she must try to convey some of this experience across the divide. This often requires challenging the assumptions that people have made about each other. The challenging may meet with hostility and a belief that the mediator is taking sides. This can put considerable strain on a relationship of trust which has been carefully nurtured over a period of time. It is therefore important that each side knows from the very beginning that the mediator is meeting with people on all sides. It is also important to set out at the beginning, and to underline frequently, the basis of the mediation: that neither side has sole possession of the truth, and that movement toward a shared reality will make possible the creation of ways to live together.

But how can you talk with those mindless murderers?

This is a question that mediators are often asked, in one form or another. It comes sometimes from opponents, who believe that the other side is inhuman, that talking with them will be futile but will give them credibility. In this case, it is important to refer again to the mediation process, and the eventual necessity of talking to, and also listening to, the other side in order to stop the killing. It will not be easy, but it will be necessary. The mediator will try to ease the process, by conveying thoughts and statements so that indirect contact can begin, and eventually (if the parties are ready) setting up confidential meetings between them. The harsh stereotypes and deep hostility will not be overcome quickly, but a beginning must be made.

The question also comes from others, not involved in the fighting, but appalled at the notion of "rewarding" violence by agreeing to talk with the perpetrators.

A Mozambican bishop who was one of the first to make contact with Renamo commented that people outside were very firm in their insistence that no such

17

contact should be made. There were two basic arguments offered. The first was that Renamo had done such unforgivable things as to put themselves beyond human reach. They were pure evil, too guilty to be allowed to be in contact with others, and too inhuman for contact to be useful. The second argument was that the situation was too urgent and too awful. Talking was too slow, and too mild a response to the slaughter of so many innocent people. The bishop persisted in making contacts, and his reasons were echoed by ordinary Mozambicans we met. Yes, the situation is dreadful, and has been for some years, and it is ordinary Mozambicans who are suffering. All avenues should be tried, including talking, in hopes that something might actually end the killing. And, yes, Renamo's activities have been awful, but one way to end this is to appeal to them, as one human being to another. If they believe they cannot be forgiven, how will they ever stop the war and rejoin society?[32]

In many situations, the people suffering most, the people being killed and having family members killed, know that they will eventually have to agree to talks with the people killing them. More than that, these ordinary, suffering people must finally accept these soldiers and guerrillas back into their midst, and get along with them on a daily basis. It is important that mediators, with fewer painful memories of suffering, should be able to bring themselves to listen and talk to all sides.

The question about "talking to mindless murderers" indicates a sense of urgency about war. There is a suspiciousness about this long-term relationship-building with leaders of armies and governments, when people are being killed every day. Why should our representatives spend time with ministers and paramilitary leaders, who may turn around the next day and order another massacre? And the mediator's answer, of course, is that if someone can find a quick solution that works well, so much the better, and everyone can stop fighting. But until that day, it is better for many people to try many methods, including mediation, to build all the components that may one day lead to an end to the killing. Mediation must not be the only approach. Someone should work with the victims of atrocities, someone with the diplomats, someone with the soldiers, someone with the paramilitaries, someone with the refugees. And, of course, it is best whenever possible to work on conflicts before the killing and the suffering begin, before bitterness and revenge make it still more difficult to rebuild the social structures that sustain peace.

Do Quakers support the mediator's "balanced partiality"?

Political figures in a polarised conflict setting are not alone in finding it hard to believe it possible to listen to someone with whom they disagree. Often, it is from the mediator's own "side", from Friends, even from the very organisation supporting the mediation work, that most questioning of this role comes. It is partly explained by another Quaker tradition, described as "speaking truth to power". Friends are often familiar with this idea, and approve of the notion that their representative holds the moral high ground, and confronts government and armies with a truth that the warring sides do not see. It is harder to accept the notion that a Quaker representative listens.

Barbara Bird: Shortly after we came to the region, we were living in Hong Kong at the time, the massacre in Tien an Men Square had occurred in June of 1989, and we came to the field in September of 1989. Approximately a year later, we went to Beijing and to other places in China, and we did that purposely. Nobody was going to China at that time. Everybody was mad, everybody was saying that you shouldn't go to China, you shouldn't talk to the Chinese. But we didn't feel that.

We went and very purposely tried to listen. We tried to meet with as many people as we could. We did not go with an agenda to criticise the Chinese for what they had done, though of course in our hearts we felt terrible. But we wanted to listen, we wanted to hear what different kinds of Chinese people would say about that event: government people, non-government, students, teachers, as many people as we could meet with. The longer we were there, and the more time we spent with individual people, the more people opened up to us. Even government people, who began to share with us: "Well, we really didn't handle that [Tien an Men Square] very well, we regret it now." But we also learned a lot about what their fears were, and why they had, maybe you could say, blundered in this way, what their anxieties were about destabilising the country. [...]

When we wrote our report, there were people who were critical because our report didn't say that we told them they shouldn't have done this, and that they were bad people, and so forth.

Sue: On the contrary, you gave <u>them</u> the chance to tell <u>you</u> that they shouldn't have done it, which is far more powerful, much more important.[33]

These Quakers found themselves challenged by other Quakers, for having listened to a range of views held by people in a difficult and unhappy situation. And the challenge is appropriate, as part of the collective testing of what is done in the corporate name. But it is also part of the mediator's sense of being always at the edge, having to justify to herself and to others the determination to stay in the middle. The belief in mediation encounters the belief in speaking truth to power, and the tension between them provides the parameters within which to act. As an individual, and as a representative of Quakers, the mediator finds the centre by continually testing the limits.

CHAPTER 4

Relationship-Building

ONE THEME RUNNING THROUGH EVERY description of this work is that its base is relationships. Necessarily, the relationships are with individuals, although an awareness of each other's function is a motivator as well: mediators may seek out leaders of specific factions or spokespeople on particular issues, and politicians may respond positively because of previous Quaker contact or because they want a channel to another side.

Analysis

The very first step is an analysis of the situation. This may be done explicitly or implicitly, but will be done often. One method is called conflict mapping, drawing an actual map of the conflict and labelling the various issues, groupings, and leaders. Other forms begin with overlapping circles or depictions of communication, influence, or interdependence. Whatever the particular method, the point is to examine the situation rigorously, looking for flash-points or points of blockage, and identifying possible points of intervention or ways to build across the divide.

Academic analyses are only one element of this process. The most important insights seem to come, not from a distance, but from people very close to the problems. The mediator finds people with all sorts of viewpoints and tests hypotheses on them. In most conflicts, there seems to be a vast, informal network of people similarly obsessed with the conflict, and willing to discuss it endlessly, from every possible standpoint, in discussion groups, pubs, and railway carriages. What is needed is precisely **not** an objective analysis, but its opposite, a kind of sum of insiders' understandings. Connections and possibilities appear unexpectedly, from casual comments and the articulation of things that everyone takes for granted. Who would have thought that the least conspicuous place for politicians from the north and south of Ireland to meet would be a rugby match? But, once it is mentioned, everyone nods and says: Of course. The mediator will find such ideas only by being completely open to possibilities, and by continually adding new dots to the map.

The map, whether physically drawn or not, will be consulted again and again. The mediator looks for indications of timing, movement, and connection, often working toward the vaguest and remotest of possible outcomes. The point is to try to offer an opening, but only an opening, knowing that the politicians and paramilitary protagonists will decide, according to their own lights, their sense of timing, and their knowledge of their own group, whether to take it up. The analysis suggests possibilities, vast numbers of shifting possibilities, and the mediator works to make a few of them become more possible.

Whom to contact

One crucial element in the analysis is the identification of points of intervention, and these points are usually people. In principle, Quakers look for the divine spark in each individual, which makes each person as worthwhile as any other. In practice, time limitations and programme objectives oblige mediators to select contacts according to criteria which are partly instrumental or judgmental, such as:

— Who is in a position of leadership or influence?
— Whom does the mediator already know or have access to?
— Whom might she[34] be introduced to by other contacts?
— Who seems frustrated by the lack of communication?
— Who seems willing to consider alternatives?
— Who is likely to be open to the process of mediation?

By these or similar criteria, the mediator will choose particular individuals on each "side" to contact, with hopes of beginning to build a relationship. In spite of this selection process, she tries to fashion relationships which value all people's experiences and views, and particularly bring into the process those groups which are left out.

The nature of the relationship

John McConnell uses Martin Buber's[35] distinction between I-thou (relating to others as equally important as oneself) and I-it (treating others as objects) to describe the kind of relationship Quaker mediators try to build:

> In mediation, what we're essentially trying to do is to transform a relationship which has degenerated into vicious I-it communication, which is destructive and causes suffering [...] into an I-thou relationship [...] with each side. From that [...] insubstantial foundation we are trying to establish a constructive dialogue sufficiently attuned to the reality of the situation for a process to take place which will result in people's lives being saved.

> People do mediate in different ways, and this effort to transform relationships may not always be the whole story, but it's a contribution that relates directly to the Quaker ethic of answering that of God in others, and it's right that we make it. Other sorts of mediation may well be quite compatible, and sometimes more effective, [...] but I feel this is the kernel of the Quaker approach.[36]

Others would use other terms, other metaphors, to describe their work, but most would find meaning in this description. This does not mean that the parties to the mediation, the politicians, soldiers, civil servants, and guerrillas, must necessarily be converted in order to participate in mediation. But Quaker mediators have in mind an I-thou relationship, a positive, life-enhancing, answering-the-divine-in-each-one sort of relationship with each individual. And they hope, in the context of that relationship, to show

21

processes and behaviours that can be used in building trust between opponents, who begin by mistrusting each other completely.

The building of these relationships takes time, commitment, openness, and flexibility. The politicians have various reasons for agreeing to an initial meeting, but they are busy people, and they maintain contact because they find it helpful, whether politically, personally, or both.

> There was one young Northern Ireland politician who had been terribly difficult at the beginning — prickly, and absolutely unwilling to venture outside the party manifesto to discuss any other possibilities at all. We met with him at intervals of several months, talking about issues as they arose, and bringing him the views of others we met. When we'd known him about two years, he suddenly looked at us one day and said: "You really do listen to all sides, don't you? When I first met you, I didn't think you would." By that time, he was markedly warmer with us, and ventured onto delicate topics himself. Later, he agreed to a meeting we offered to arrange with his counterpart in another party, with an agenda limited to a fairly non-controversial area. Some months later, he cheerfully agreed to meet someone from a very different party, whom we had expected him to be reluctant to meet with. We had by then known him for about three years.
>
> Our relationship with him proceeded steadily, from guarded sessions about party positions, to candid discussions of ways to improve the political process, and including the sharing of rather personal views of the world and the importance of politics from a religious perspective. We moved very slowly in suggesting that he meet with others, and he never refused or expressed regret.
>
> But the trust between us does not seem altogether personal. Though we have shared and found agreement on some fairly profound issues, it is not an intimate friendship. The relationship seems to be based on his having tested us according to what we described as our function, and found us trustworthy. Perhaps more surprisingly, he found the function itself useful. Before meeting us, he would not have expressed a need for someone to bring him other views or set up meetings across the divides, but he has found this useful. And there is a good chance that successors in this role would find him willing to give them a chance to earn his trust.[37]

Each relationship is unique, of course, but this pattern is probably as likely as any other. Over time, as the parties get to know each other, they are able to become more human with each other, and to fashion links that are trusted and resilient.

How does the mediator get started?

The first stage is introductions. The Quaker representative begins by contacting a political figure, paramilitary, rebel leader, or civil servant. Some contacts are "inherited" from predecessors; these will recognise Quakers and may even understand what the role is about. With others, one begins by writing a letter, describing the role in terms of understanding positions and facilitating communication, and seeking an initial meeting. It turns out to be useful to perfect a one- or two-sentence description of the role, understanding that many people will have questions to ask, while others will simply wait and see.

It should be emphasised that most Quaker representatives would not describe themselves as mediators. They might call themselves reconcilers or facilitators of communication or people who represent certain values in a particular situation. So, in introducing themselves, the word mediator would not be used. It may be that, as the relationship develops, the Quaker may be drawn into a kind of mediating role. But that has to come gradually, as trust and credibility increase. As Sydney Bailey says:

> I have never actually offered to mediate but I do try to make it clear that I want to understand more about the problems, that I would like to help, and that I am in touch with the other side.[38]

Sometimes, one may be introduced by a local person, and inherit some of this person's credibility. In conflict situations, the issue is likely to be an important one, because trust is not automatically extended to unknown people.

Steve: Are there particular factors that would lead people to accept you immediately, or to feel hostile?

John McConnell: I think one factor that's important is how we are introduced. [...] How do they come to know about us? Do they see us as coming essentially at the behest of the other side? Have we perhaps insinuated ourselves in a way which could in the claustrophobic environment of conflict lead to suspicion? Or does someone whom they trust actively introduce us and vouch for our integrity of purpose?[39]

The credibility described in Chapter 2 is really only a beginning: an important first hurdle, which will determine whether one gets to try the rest of the hurdles, but only the first one. Then come actual meetings, and one begins to be judged by one's own words and actions.

First meetings are often limited to the promulgation of the party line. Like the rest of us, politicians keep repeating themselves until they are sure they've been heard. In these abnormal, polarised situations, it is difficult to believe that anyone will listen to more than one side. So, they begin with formal statements, expecting to be met with either agreement or hostility. As in the Northern Ireland example cited above, the politician's initial defensiveness or desire to convert yields, with time, to a more complex relationship. The Quaker's careful listening and checking, seeking of experiences behind the political positions, and gradual introduction of different views and experiences, help to build a relationship that may enable the politician to take the next step. The next step must be one that appears naturally, as an outgrowth of the relationship in the context of larger events, but not as a manipulation of trust.

Joel McClellan: I've had a good relationship with the Chinese ambassador and a very good relationship with some of the people who work on the

Tibet issue. And I've kept that going for some time... I feel a strong responsibility that something should be done there, but I haven't a clue what to do. So I just carry on going to a nice tea with the Chinese ambassador, and meeting the lovely people who are tied up with the Dalai Lama. [...]

Steve Williams: Is that the sort of thing you would be inclined to take to a committee as a concern, as something that should be pursued?

Joel: I think I would wait until there are further developments along the way, until I saw something, some opening.

Steve: While it's still at the stage of relationships, it would seem almost exploitative to go to a committee and say, I have a good relationship, so let's push him to do something.[40]

Because Quakers undertake this work as a living out of religious faith, they may be freer than most to be patient, to wait for a way to open. The long-term commitment, either to live in a situation or to keep coming back over a period of years, allows relationships to develop naturally, without having to push individuals or groups into doing something. But the Quaker representative feels the responsibility to remain alert to openings, and to facilitate new possibilities at the earliest possible moment.

The testing stage

Usually the first, and most explicit, form of testing is whether the potential mediator actually has contacts that might be useful. It is necessary to indicate that one talks with people from other sides, understands something of their views, and has channels for conveying ideas or arranging meetings. At the same time, confidentiality means that not much can be said about specific individuals. And, realistically, if the mediator throws people's names around lightly, the new contact is likely to expect that his own name will be similarly bandied about. It is helpful to describe a range of contacts, affirming that there is a circle in which communication needs to be restored, but not readily attributing specific statements to individuals.

As well as contacts, there is testing of content. In an apparently general conversation about events of the day, there will be quiet vigilance to see what bias is coming through. There may also be quite explicit comparison with what the politician hears from other sources. Since the point of the whole exercise is that there is not enough communication between the sides, the politician's ideal is to hear things which are consistent with what other sources say, but go beyond it. He may be particularly interested in only one or two viewpoints, but mediators often describe a wide range of views, reasserting the belief that all must be considered.

Assurances of confidentiality are usually the last to be tested, at least explicitly, but they must be proven before anything delicate will be entrusted to this channel.

And then another factor is confidentiality. We are going into a situation which might be life and death for the conflictants, and they have to know they can trust us. But how do they know that? Unless we have a very good pedigree, unless the conflictants already know and trust someone who is already part of the situation - I'm thinking of John Paul Lederach's description of how "confianza" contributed to mediation initiatives in Nicaragua – how can they trust us? So, inevitably, a certain amount of probing goes on.

On one occasion, we were given really sensitive information – the stuff of headlines – that a guerrilla leader had been killed by his own army, and we were told this was confidential. Actually it wasn't true – we later met the man – and it is well within the bounds of plausibility that this distinctive piece of information should be given to us to discover whom we consulted and whether we spoke to journalists.[41]

Meanwhile, the mediator is also doing some testing: in a sharing of views about the current situation, what does the politician want to have conveyed, and to whom? In short-term initiatives, it is perhaps easier to be clear and explicit about the specific message and its target. In a residential model of long-term relationship-building, there will sometimes be specific messages: but, more often, the mediator will test her understanding of views, pick up clues about targets and attribution, and often use intuition to sense what is intended. She may suggest that a particular individual might be interested in this view, or bring back responses to previous statements, and use the politician's reactions to understand his intentions. Each such exchange helps to build a picture of what each has in mind, and at the same time builds the relationship.

Becoming familiar with each other

The mere passage of time seems to be important in the development of these relationships. This is partly because people in conflict situations have often had negative experiences of journalists, academics, or other visitors becoming "experts" in a few days, or even coming with elaborate solutions. One-off workshops and conferences can leave the organisers free to return home to write an article, whether the conference attenders have gained something from the meetings, or have simply ended up in greater danger.

The time spent with people as well as tangible expressions of concern for their physical needs are both factors in gaining their confidence, as described here by one Quaker mediator:

In the initial stages I spent a lot of time with them. I would sit on the seashore or in the garden and eat the same food as they were eating, so that they would feel that I am with them. And [I was] not only talking about the peace process but making sure that their immediate needs were being met. Some of the medical help that we gave the refugees played a very important part in that.[42]

The simple commitment of staying on or coming back many times does seem to have an impact. One is able to demonstrate a concern for the people as well as the process, and eventually able to meet people without artificial structures or special arrangements.

One of the clear advantages to being residential, at least in the Northern Ireland situation, is that we could make ourselves available in places where people would find us in a more natural way than us having to seek them out or them having to seek us out.

We would attend political party conferences, city council meetings, other kinds of gatherings where we could expect to find the key politicians, or where they could expect to find us. And if they had something they wanted to talk to us about, they could find us in a more natural setting, and not have to come to our house or make a special arrangement to see us.

If there was something worth pursuing, then we could arrange to meet them again later. But I think it just made them aware that we're here, whenever they need us, and they would see us in a variety of settings, our faces became familiar to them.[43]

In addition, being present over time gives the Quaker representative a context in which to see present actions and statements, and a vision of where things might be leading. Politicians under pressure change very slowly, if at all. And their public statements usually lag far behind their private views: they are reluctant to express disagreement with their own group, or moderation in their views toward the other side, for fear of being seen as traitors.

One of the difficulties that I often find with people who come into a situation to mediate, negotiate, or what-have-you, is that they come in at a horizontal time-slice. There's no sense of synchronicity, and therefore they don't know where people were in the past. They don't know what the trajectory looks like, and therefore really don't have a sense of where you might urge them to go.[44]

The mediator who has long experience of the situation and is familiar with the individuals will be able to see possibilities, encourage movement, and applaud it when it occurs. The confidential process will enable the political leader to try out possible shifts in his own attitude, and get reactions from his own group as well as opponents, before making a public change.

Relationships as commitment

Some mediation has been done by Quakers who live in the situation or move there for a period of years, some by people who come for visits of several weeks, over a period of years. In either case, there is a long-term commitment, ideally by both the individual and the supporting organisation, that they expect to maintain their concern about the situation and do what they can to help. Of course, circumstances do change, but the relationships and the nature of the process commit one to a serious undertaking that must be sustained if it can be.

I've seen maybe half a dozen organisations which have tried to get involved in mediation, talked with one or both sides, and then have given up. [...]

People might, obviously, not keep with it to the end, but if an organisation gets involved with it, I think you've got to hang on almost to the end. [...]

26

You can't say we lay it down when everything is hopeless, you can't say we lay it down when one side seems to be dominant over the other, unless it's finished.

I do know that you've got to be on for the long ride. This is not something that, because you've got access to the president and he's willing to see you, and then you go back to the militants and they say this, then you can just go. That's not what it's about. Access is one thing, but to really establish that trust takes a much longer time. And then you're committed. Once you've established that trust, how can you tell someone who trusts you, "I'm sorry, but I can't have anything more to do with this".[45]

Because the work is about relationships, and not just functions, it bears a greater long-term obligation. Someone who supplies a machine part or a cleaning service may decide to retire, and simply announce this to his customers, perhaps recommending a replacement. A mediator who has built human relationships, and who serves perhaps a unique function in being a direct link between implacable opponents, must take seriously the need to sustain the relationships for as long as possible, and make appropriate arrangements for continuity at the time of departure.

Handing on/handing over

Often, particularly in non-residential mediation efforts, there are "teams" of people working together, two or three of whom may be able to go on each visit. Over the years, these individuals meet often, discuss every aspect of the situation, reach decisions collectively, and work very closely together. If one must be replaced, continuity may not be a great problem, because the others remain the same. In addition, the relationships with each political or military leader have, from the beginning, been somewhat collective relationships; certain individuals may hit it off better than others, but they have learned to know and trust in each other in the context of a team. The relationship with the new member can be established gradually, under the auspices of people who are already known and trusted, and with relatively little dislocation. Still, there is a need to take care that there is sufficient continuity and communication between team members, so that each knows what has happened.

Sue: Do you have a sense of whether these [approaches to doing mediation] are transferable from one person to another? Have the members of the teams learned things from each other as they've gone along? Can you incorporate a new person easily? [...]

Ram: The thing is transferable, but it is not direct theoretical transfer. It is a combination of things — combination of words, of behaviour, of circumstances, of ability to go as low as possible in order to listen to different people without standing on certain formalities, without feeling humiliated. These things will only come, or even sensitivity: we talk about sensitivity, but this sensitivity very often is not easily definable. This only comes when you see how other people are reacting. Now, when you ask, "Is it transferable, is it

27

possible?", I can only say this much. I have personally gained by visits in the initial stages with [two more experienced members of the team]. There are many areas where I learned. I have gained a considerable amount from such visits. [...] If a mediation is going on and this is to be continued, then you must induct somebody in while you are there. Unless you can induct somebody in and continually do this together, it will be very difficult.[46]

When there is a team of people making visits together, it is possible for new people to work over a period of time with those who have been involved longer. In residential posts, on the other hand — with resident representatives or Quakers mediating in the places where they already live — there are usually only one or two people involved, who come at the same time and depart at the same time, to be replaced by someone new. Relationships may be or seem to be more personal, more dependent on the particular individuals, and thus more difficult to hand on to new people. The handover period is often very short, and in any case often involves introducing someone who is entirely unfamiliar with the situation. The new representative, then, cannot concentrate only on relationships, but must develop an understanding of the conflict and the parties to it, before being able to build relationships with leaders of the sides.

The experience has been that what the new representative inherits is the opportunity to be tested. Politicians, government people, and armed groups will generally agree to a first meeting with the new person, and will not need much briefing about what is intended, but they will need to make their own decisions about whether to trust this new individual.

If there is a sensitive person that comes into this position, contacts will be open to them. If they're not, then they won't. But it's an individual gaining the respectability, and not an organisation.[47]

The organisation acts as the guarantor of collective testing and of a corporate commitment of resources. The organisational link to the previous representatives earns the first meeting and a positive predisposition. But the process depends on relationships, and those must be built between particular human beings.

There are, of course, sensible things to do in preparing to hand over a mediating role to a successor. She should certainly read a great deal about the current situation and its history. She should have access to reports of conferences and meetings arranged by predecessors, as well as other reports or analyses written by them. There should be some time of overlap, so departing representatives can introduce new people. During this time, old hands can also act as a sounding-board for newcomers, helping them to understand the nuances of the situation and the unstated messages communicated by various sides.

The nature of the work is likely to change somewhat, both because of the new people and because the situation itself changes over time. All the more reason, then, for new representatives to be as clear as possible about what their predecessors were doing, as this is where the parties will expect them to start. All parties should be clear that new

Quaker representatives are individuals, and as such will be different. But they are still part of the same organisation, still subject to collective guidance, still committed to the same approaches and processes. Changes of personnel need not undo everything that has been done. Ideally, the new representatives will learn from what has been done before, and improve upon it.

CHAPTER 5

Building Trust

IF IT BECOMES POSSIBLE TO BUILD relationships with some of the important actors at different levels of a political conflict, what happens next? The relationship is its own justification and reward, as all human relationships are opportunities to see another viewpoint, hear another truth, and be touched by another's spirit. In some way, the relationship can be neither a means nor an end. It will lose its integrity if it is approached instrumentally, if the mediator cultivates people because she sees them as useful to her: this is Martin Buber's I-it approach.

But it would also seem false to seek out political acquaintances in order simply to "relate" to them: they have expressed no need for this friendship, so the relationship would seem to be meeting some need of the mediator's only. It is no accident that mediators are so often confronted at the beginning with questions about their intentions. Motives for doing mediation will be considered in more depth in a later chapter, but it should be said here that motives and intentions are a factor in the mediator's ability to build trust.

If the intention is not simply to relate, but to relate with some purpose, what seems appropriate is a working relationship, aimed at a shared goal of improving communication and modifying a destructive political process, but a working relationship conducted with particular care for the building of trust between opponents.

Facing a trusted person first

One of the mediator's goals is for people who are bent on killing each other to talk together and listen to each other instead. Issuing the invitation is not enough. The process of building trust between adversaries is often long, slow, and delicate. Long before they are ready to negotiate, they may try the mediation process separately, trusting the mediator enough to allow her to stand in for the other side.

During our time in Belfast, we had some kind of ongoing relationship with over 70 political figures (I counted them one day, out of curiosity) at various levels of different parties and groupings. Many of these relationships, about half, remained fairly functional: cordial, but focused on arranging one particular meeting or communicating with one individual or side. These politicians still seemed to have questions: Are these people trying to use me? Can they be useful to me?

Nearly half the relationships, it seemed to me, achieved a degree of transparency. That is, the politician had tested us as intermediaries, and perhaps also as people, had decided what the purpose of our joint meetings was, and knew us well enough to take us for granted. He began to look through us, and see instead the opponent he wanted to talk to or hear from.

I felt it very strongly, for example, at one meeting in Dublin, with a particular party leader and the party spokesman on Northern Ireland. Perhaps it seems especially vivid because they asked us a barrage of questions about different Northern parties and groupings, one after the other. As we switched from describing one set of views to another, the two men across the table changed their facial expressions, posture, tone of voice, and debating strategy, reflecting how they would approach each group. It was as though we offered them a practice session, a chance to rehearse a meeting with several different sides in turn.[48]

This is one sense in which shuttle mediation — going back and forth between different sides — is mediation proper: the mediator may go through the full mediation process with two sides separately, before they become willing to try the process together. This gives them a chance to build some trust in the process, before facing each other. Mediators in other polarised situations, including the Middle East, have had experiences similar to this.

Unilateral actions

In situations of continuing violence and polarisation, and particularly where there is a history of betrayal or failed attempts at mediation, one or both sides may refuse completely to consider negotiating or even communicating with the other side. Instead, one side will sometimes decide on a unilateral action, which does not depend on the other side at all, and wait to see what the response is. The role of the mediator will then be to help each side to notice and interpret the other's action, while both insist that there is no communication between them.

For example, in recent years, all cease-fires in Northern Ireland have been unilateral, initiated by a paramilitary group. Sometimes the Republicans declare a cease-fire, and the Loyalists decide whether to follow suit or not; sometimes the Loyalists announce one, and the Republicans also suspend their armed actions, or do not; in any case, the government does not formally recognise it or respond. Mediators may be consulted by one or more sides, to make clear what it can look for as a reply. "How will they recognise your response?" is a useful question, committing no one to actual negotiation or even communication, but offering the opportunity to string unilateral acts together to lead somewhere.

Indirect communication

If unilateral actions begin to demonstrate to each side the other's authentic interest in change, a degree of good faith, and some ability to control its agents, a new stage may be reached. It may now be possible to begin moving toward direct communication, or at least acknowledging the need for indirect communication. This, too, is a careful, step-by-step process, with each side weighing carefully what it is prepared to risk on each step. This process is used by individuals, often leaders of groupings, to get a better sense of the opponent and the possible outcome of talks before leading his group into direct negotiations. A politician may perceive that he has much to lose, and that his constituency and the political process both favour inertia, standing pat. An incremental process offers the opportunity to make small steps, and reconsider after each one.

Over a period of about two years, we went back and forth between one party leader and the main advisor to another party leader. The advisor had everything to gain in meeting directly, the leader everything to lose, and both seemed to understand this. At first, they gave us party positions, then clarifications of positions, and later a general sharing of views. Eventually, each side designated someone close but not officially connected with them, for a direct meeting and exploration of issues. Later, each began to suggest changes and proposals. Then, the two party leaders started giving us copies of their public speeches, highlighting phrases that were public changes inspired by their indirect communication. Finally, as part of more formal process, they began to meet directly.[49]

The small increments allowed for the slow, careful establishment of a small but growing degree of trust in the process, and perhaps in the opponent.

As this example suggests, the process is often a long and delicate one. There are incidents which derail it: constituency pressures, changes in dominant faction, threats to leadership, public statements by others, and influences of all sorts. The people involved are pragmatic politicians, determined to increase their own and their party's power. They engage in this kind of step-by-step movement toward communication with the opponent only if the likely benefits seem to outweigh the risks. And it is not their only strategy.

My feeling constantly was that they are sincere in working with us, but that's one of several alternatives. And success could be a total military victory, success could be a negotiated settlement, or something in the middle. There is a sincerity in their saying things to us, even while they're waging a campaign and getting new gunboats.[50]

Joe Elder reflects here one of the mediator's own anxieties, as he tries to reconcile his sense that his contacts are "sincere" in talking with him about ways to end a war, with the knowledge that they are continuing to wage that war at the same time. The mediator may have rejected armed violence, but she deals with people who have not, people leading groups which may trust guns much more than people.

The mediator comes to know civil servants, politicians, leaders of armed groups, and diplomats, relating to them perhaps on a deeply human level, and seeking to encourage their positive, creative, constructive capacities. But these people are and remain practical, hard-headed actors in a painful, often violent conflict. It is not helpful to depend too heavily on their idealism and their trust. These aspects are there, but side by side with a pragmatic, calculating assessment of the risks and possibilities in the situation. To be useful to them, mediation must offer a realistic chance of success in their terms: reducing suffering by their own people, without giving up fundamental needs or showing them as traitors to their own side.

Building trust between warring sides is, of course, not a simple business, though there are people who offer simplistic answers, such as "If A and B both trust me, they will then come to trust each other," or "If I can get them to use my model, they will see they can trust it and then get on with negotiating," or "When I tell them about this comparable situation in Switzerland and my clever adaptation to solve their problem, everything will be fine." The experience of Quaker mediators is that an acceptable mediator, a useful process, and some creative alternatives are helpful, but even together they are not enough. People finally solve their own conflicts, using everything they can find or invent, and depending on issues of timing and the flow of events that none of us can control.

Sue Williams: But you keep negotiating, again trying to build a path, or help them build a path, that will lead somewhere else than what is already the obvious choice. And that's an important role. You can't lay out the path for them.

Joe Elder: Yes, because it's sort of step-by-step. You move, and they move, and so on. Several times, all the pieces seemed to be there, if you could just get the right combination of people, and have no incident which either side could use as the great excuse: "We were betrayed".[51]

The politicians are always aware of the possibilities for things to go wrong. They seem, as a group, more naturally cautious than optimistic. Perhaps Quakers, who come with a seemingly endless source of idealism and optimism, act as a foil, and appeal to something hidden in the politicians. But both groups recognise that politicians are at much greater risk than mediators, have to contend with more factors, and pay a higher price for a failed initiative. Mediators and politicians come to have respect for each other, in their very different roles. But the mediator must understand that it will take considerable trust, for members of political parties or armed groups to consider not only talking to, but actually listening to, someone they see as the enemy.

Another aspect of the question of dealing with "killers" has to do with our fear that, if we listen to a viewpoint, and do not challenge it, we will be seen somehow to have accepted it. I have learned to be patient about that. Most of us don't listen until we are sure we have been heard. So, I listen to politicians or paramilitary groups talk for a long time, and make sure I understand their viewpoint before I bring in others. That is important, for it is what I am asking of them. I am asking them to meet with someone from another side, to listen to a person they know they disagree with, to try to understand and move toward a process of reconciliation.[52]

The aim of this relationship is not the relationship itself, but the possibility that the trust established here might lead to the beginnings of trust between the opponents. For that shift to happen, the mediator must be looking for opportunities to bring the opponents together.

CHAPTER 6

Bringing the Sides Together

IN BUILDING RELATIONSHIPS WITH PEOPLE on all sides, the Quaker mediator is looking for opportunities to bring these parties together, or at least closer to each other, in a way that might lead to better understanding and peace.[53] The most important relationships to build are those between the parties in conflict. As was stated before, many of the Quaker representatives who fill this role would not describe themselves as mediators, but rather as facilitators or reconcilers. In some cases, they have offered this function when requested, but see their work as being primarily something else.

Not yet together

The Quaker United Nations Offices (QUNO) in New York and Geneva are places where this role sometimes comes into play. Stephen Collett of the New York office gives this example:

> We have, for over 15 years, kept contact with the missions of both North and South Korea. There you are certainly facilitating a dialogue at second hand. They do not speak to each other. But that work has come so far that recently we sponsored an all day, off-the-record meeting at Quaker House where representatives of both the North and South came - one in the morning and one in the afternoon - to speak to a committee of Quakers about their perspectives on the situation in Korea.[54]

Here is a case of bringing the sides closer to each other, but not directly together. The hope is that this kind of "second-hand" contact will lead the sides to more direct contact.

Peter Herby, a staff member in QUNO-Geneva, has focused on the specific process of arms negotiations. When he first came to QUNO, he realised that he wasn't building relationships for some distant point in the future, but in order to have influence on the more immediate process of negotiation. When the process of arms negotiation in Geneva was stuck, he sensed that a separate process happening in Stockholm was a place to have influence with negotiators to help bring the process back on track. He describes his role as "conciliation".[55] And from all reports of the off-the-record meetings that he organised in Stockholm, they did, in fact, allow some of the negotiators to meet and discuss issues in a non-threatening atmosphere that was very helpful to the more formal and public negotiations process.

Direct meetings
      At various levels, Quaker representatives based in many places have found opportunities to bring people from different sides together around various issues, or sometimes just to allow them to meet and begin to form a direct relationship with each other. An example from Sri Lanka shows that attempts to bring people together may demand considerable patience and perseverance.

> When we first went to Jaffna, we spoke to the churches, both Catholic and Protestant. The churches were divided, both north and south, on ethnic lines. And I used to ask them: "There is only one community that can bring north and south together, and that is the Christian community. You may be Protestant, you may be Catholic, but both are, both claim to be Christ's people. You have got people in the south who are also Christ's people. How is it that you cannot come together? How is it that you cannot find in your own theological studies something to trigger that unity?" Somehow, it didn't work. [...]
>
> Whenever we went, we [...] kept telling [Christians in the south] that they should visit [the north]. Then we had to tell the people in the north, "You should help these people to visit." They were talking to their own groups and they welcomed the people from the south to come. And it happened just a year ago. After 9 years, it has happened. But it is a slow process. I'm not saying that I was responsible for it.
>
> We said the same thing to the Buddhist monks. Buddhist Sinhalese monks went to the north and came back. They had been afraid of going because they thought the [Tamil] Tigers would kill them. When we spoke to them, they asked us, "Let us know what the Tigers say about this." They [the Tigers] said to us, "We welcome anybody who wants to come and have a look at this place. Let them come." And they [the Buddhist monks] did.[56]

These kinds of direct meetings are preceded by months or even years of relationship-building and indirect communication through various channels, including the Quaker representatives. The level of trust that a Quaker mediator has established with the individuals is what allows her to make the suggestion or invitation for the parties to meet.

> During our first two years in Belfast, we formed relationships with quite a wide range of people in all the political parties. As it happened, we had a good relationship by this time with two younger politicians, one from a nationalist party and one from a unionist party. They were about the same age and had similar positions in their respective parties - both working on similar policy issues and both being close advisors to their own party leaders. It was a time when the possibility of direct political negotiations was under discussion, but

there were some difficulties between their two parties about the basis and agenda for these negotiations.

We suggested to each of these people separately that they consider meeting in an off-the-record way to discuss some areas of common concern, as well as some of the differences. They both agreed to meet at our invitation, with the understanding that neither could be seen as representing his own party in any kind of negotiations.

The meeting took place in our house in a comfortable sitting room in front of a turf fire. One of them arrived early and we talked with him about current issues before the second person arrived. He was not as relaxed as he had usually been with us, no doubt because he was nervous about the meeting about to happen. We asked if there were particular concerns or issues that he wanted to raise. He referred to a strong statement made on the radio that morning by a member of the other's party. The statement had essentially been a condemnation of his own party for an action they had taken. He felt that this could make his own meeting with the other person quite tense and uncomfortable.

The other politician arrived and apologised for being late. We introduced them to each other and they began to talk about the fact that they had been at university at the same time, but had never met. The conversation was somewhat stiff and superficial for a while, as they edged toward more substantive issues. Eventually, as the effect of the turf fire and a cup of tea seemed to relax them a bit, they talked in some depth about the particular areas of party policies that they were working on.

The issue of the strong statement on the radio that morning was referred to and acknowledged, but not dwelt on. They talked of the agenda and possible basis for inter-party talks, each stating his own party's views more fully than was usual, and clarifying the other party's views, but with the clear understanding that neither of them was empowered to negotiate.

After the meeting ended, they walked out together, and continued to talk for a while on the footpath outside the house. It was our impression that they had further, direct contact afterward, and they agreed to sit on a panel together.[57]

In this kind of direct meeting, the role of the mediator has changed. The trust she has established with the two people reassures them that the meeting can happen without publicity, and the presence of the third party may be essential for the meeting to occur. In this case, it was particularly important to one of the parties that the meeting be at the invitation of the mediators, as his own side would not tolerate his either seeking or accepting an invitation from someone on the other side. In each other's presence, the opponents may need the mediator's help in getting started, but usually prefer to concentrate on each other, with little or no intervention. Often, having been introduced and exchanged telephone numbers, individuals will want only one or two meetings under the auspices of the third party, and then they prefer to contact each other directly and arrange their own meetings.

An example from another part of the world illustrates a situation where people concerned with the same issues had never actually met each other, though there was no particular reason that they couldn't meet. The assistance of interested, sensitive outsiders in bringing them together once was all that was necessary to initiate a process in which they continued to meet regularly after that. The situation is in Hong Kong, and the people concerned are all involved in some way with the Vietnamese "boat people". The interested outsiders are the Quaker International Affairs Representatives in the region. One of them describes the scenario:

> Well, we met with some of the people who had been working with those issues for a long time and tried to identify a wish-list of people who would be involved, and then a reality list. We talked together about who could approach whom in which ways, just standard straight-forward kinds of ways, and exploited all of the possible connections that there were, and said, "Hey, would you be interested in hearing what these guys think for a few hours one afternoon?" Put the right way, through the right people with the right introductions, there wasn't any particular reason for people not to say yes.
>
> Two or three things were particularly helpful about it. One of them was that we were total outsiders and didn't know any of the participants, and everybody said "Oh, I've never met you before, and you're not one of the designated fools." And it really made a tremendous difference in whether people were willing to talk to us and could believe that we didn't have any axe to grind. So it was very easy in that way.
>
> We just put together a very light easy way of thinking about how the discussion might go, that invited people from the various parties to say why they were interested in meeting the other people there, and to say what they hoped to get out of it. It just took care of itself, in giving people a chance to raise the questions that you knew people would raise if you had talked with them a little and gotten a little of their viewpoint. And so it was just one of those easy things when what you hoped would be aired was, but in especially vivid, interesting ways, that there was no way to count on. I remember one of the Vietnamese people saying about half way through it, "Well, the next time I hear you saying some dumb thing on TV, I'll remember that it was you. What you've just said sounds pretty reasonable".
>
> People said things like that because it never occurred to them to just sit and talk, because the situation was so polarized and so committed. They thought they knew what all the issues were and they were very, very tightly held. So when people said "I'm interested because...", the "because" tended to strike on a lot of shared ground. It was just a classic example of having cartoon views of other people. Not that they weren't terrible issues, because they were, but they were held at a cartoon kind of level.
>
> One of the things that happened from that meeting was the formation of a working group that continues to be very active and has been responsible for the development of some community-based refugee camps that aren't like prison-run things with little cells. So it just was one of those wonderful, serendipitous events.[58]

38

Wouldn't it be nice if all attempts to bring people together went so smoothly? Sometimes it seems that people are able to connect with each other very quickly in a way that transforms the I-it relationship into an I-thou relationship, to repeat John McConnell's reference to Martin Buber. It is very satisfying for the facilitator or mediator when this happens. And it can be quite a revelation for the parties involved, to realise suddenly that the person they hated or opposed is not all bad or the personification of evil, but rather has reasons for what he believes, and has some ideas that actually make sense.

Together, but apart

There will be many times, of course, when people will come together, but will not connect so quickly or easily. In conflicts with a long history of violence and counter-violence, the sides will not be so likely to see anything reasonable in what the other person is saying. In fact, they may not even be willing to hear what the other side has to say. Brewster Grace describes the Quaker experience of bringing Arabs and Israelis together to discuss arms control:

> We have had some Arab government officials attend a conference during which they refused to attend a particular meeting where a former commander of the Israeli armed forces was talking. But still they came to the conference. (This, in our minds, is a result of ongoing contacts and goodwill.) These conferences have been, in effect, a contribution to promoting dialogue among Arab and Israeli experts on arms control. And by bringing the Arabs and Israelis together, we find that the opinions among the participants are beginning to get closer, and it is becoming easier for them to discuss the issues.[59]

Trust in the process, to bring change

Occasionally, opposing leaders develop a certain trust in each other, and this relationship enables them to change and to take their groups with them. More often, trust is developed in the process rather than the individual — trust in the mediation process and, ultimately, in the political process that will be developed and refined through negotiations and over time.

The protocol of polarised politics is such that people whose groups are not in direct contact feel unable to build a link between themselves. But they may be able to meet each other at a conference or in the presence of a third party, and eventually allow a channel to be established that connects them directly. Once established, this link can sometimes be re-activated by them, without a need for the third party, and the mediator has the satisfaction of having worked herself out of a job. On the mediator's part, as well, it takes some trust in the process.

> It does take a kind of trust, in conferences and meetings, to bring them together and recognise that some of the most important interactions will take place without you. They will send you off to write up the memo, while they have the important discussions over lunch. You were useful in bringing them together,

but they don't want you in charge of the dialogue. And you have to accept that, and be pleased with that.[60]

All of these stages require change, the willingness to be a bit vulnerable, and the taking of risks. Yet one expects all this to be done by hard-headed politicians and guerrilla leaders whose groups are reluctant to trust the "other" at all. It is, therefore, vital that mediators have realistic expectations of what the individual and the relationship can bear.

Mediators learn to accept the need for small increments of change, and they sustain their commitment to relationships, even when groups or individuals within them appear to have done terrible things. If initiatives fail, the mediator may be disowned; if they succeed, the mediator will not expect public credit, and will feel successful if she is no longer needed as a channel. The relationship is based on this understanding, and she will remain committed to it through any of these possibilities. And the mediator is also likely to be changed by the relationships: to put oneself in the middle is to open oneself to the possibility of transformation.

CHAPTER 7

The Roles of a Quaker Representative

THE QUAKER REPRESENTATIVE BUILDS relationships of trust that can eventually lead to the facilitation of direct meetings between people in conflict with each other. This may happen over a long period of time, in the course of which a variety of functions might be served through these relationships. Many of these kinds of work seem to be common to mediation and Quaker representation; a few particular activities present special problems or opportunities.

General areas of work

The possible roles seem to include the following general areas and types of activities:

Work on **communication**, including:

— clarifying misunderstandings, both verbal messages and actions;

— asking innocent questions;

— interpreting fears, hopes and intentions of members of different groups to one another;

— message-carrying;

— help in assessing responses or predicting likely reactions by other sides to own messages/actions;

— work within a "side," for internal unity and confidence;

— maintaining contact with excluded or marginalised voices;

Pollination:

— testing possibilities (without attribution);

— collecting and distributing views around the broken circle of participants;

— drawing attention to facts that might have been overlooked by the parties involved;

— developing texts of agreed points or possible options;

— introducing a new or wider perspective, perhaps ideas that have been tried elsewhere;

Confidant:
— listening;
— empathy;
— bringing up/responding to moral values;
— speculating about possibilities;
— applauding/encouraging movement toward moderation, creativity, or risk-taking;
— supporting and strengthening efforts at achieving a just settlement in a conciliatory manner;
— commiserating;

Reconciliation:
— erosion of stereotypes;
— relationship-building with politicians;
— setting up conferences and other opportunities for people to meet in the presence of others;
— arranging direct meetings between opponents;
— building empathy and eventually relationships between opponents.

Conferences

Sometimes, initial meetings may be arranged as conferences or academic seminars. These are opportunities for political leaders to come together in the safety of a group meeting with a particular agenda; at an early stage, the agenda often has to do with the common ground rather than the most divisive issues, which they would not yet be able to confront together. In meeting, participants begin to hear each other's viewpoints and to get to know each other, though they may not yet be ready to meet one-on-one. The Quaker representative facilitates this process by having good relationships with individuals on all sides, offering a neutral venue and the ground-rule that participants will not be quoted, and responding flexibly to make the meeting as fruitful as possible for participants.

At a meeting two or three years ago in Holland, I'd known half of each of the Israeli and the Palestinian groups. At one point, they'd been having one of these classic arguments. They'd each misstated positions, and they were in confrontation.

And the group decided, all right, let's back off, and we'll get a small group to see if they can re-state the rest of the agenda. They did that, and they asked if I would join them. There was a little discussion, and then it got close to lunchtime, and the Israeli and the Palestinian each said: Everett, why don't you draft the statement for us? And then went off to lunch.

And it was said, half in jest, and half because I'm fairly good at quickly taking people's ideas and putting them in summary form. And the assumption on both sides was that they knew me well enough, they knew they weren't going to get caught out or get embarrassed.[61]

This work builds on other Quaker work, across time and space. The credibility and the contacts may depend on earlier conferences, joint undertakings with current representatives in other places, or related development or relief work.

Quaker representatives who arrange conferences often become known over time for their·expertise in particular areas, as well as for their broad contacts and credibility. As representatives develop relationships of trust with a range of politicians, academics, diplomats, and technical experts, they are able to bring groups of them together to consider specific issues.

> In terms of the actual reconciliation, that is, having the people together, we have more of a niche at the higher level of politics than we do at the level of local politics. And this is where an important part of Quaker International Affairs Representative work comes into play. Because we have a level of credibility, and we have diplomatic contacts, and all that, and we've been able to cooperate with Peter Herby [of the Quaker United Nations Office] in Geneva, and we've been able to bring technical expertise into the region, and build up a reputation. So arms control has become very important.[62]

In this case, the expertise of Quakers was in arms control and disarmament. In Northern Ireland, it is recognised that a number of Quakers have considerable experience and expertise in relation to prisons and prisoners. In another situation, it may be that specific Quakers have expertise in refugee or development work. At conferences and gatherings arranged by Quaker representatives, they try to link those who have technical expertise with others who have actual first-hand experience in a way that reflects a commitment to airing all sides of the particular issue.

Shuttle mediation

The mediator is an unusual audience in a polarised situation: someone who is not committed to any one side, but is knowledgeable about politics, and in contact with a wide range of people. Some mediators offer their own views on the events of the day, while others limit themselves to bringing the views of other parties to the conflict. In either case, this may be more direct political dialogue and debate than the politician ordinarily experiences, particularly if his is an armed group or for other reasons not usually included in the political forum.

Over time, the mediator hopes to complete the broken circle of communication, bringing each person the views and experiences of people with whom he is not in direct contact. Sometimes this means the interpretation of fears, hopes and intentions between sides that lack trust in each other, but are willing to trust the mediator. This indirect communication may lead to attempts to understand and even predict the reactions of others, and then to requests to carry messages or set up direct meetings.

A note of caution is needed about this role, as there is a danger that indirect communication could be distorted by the mediator or misinterpreted by the recipient.

It is when parties do not communicate directly that the intermediary is most needed, but this is when there is the risk that the intermediary will unwittingly distort the message. [...] Certainly, an intermediary who wants to be trusted should avoid selecting or manipulating information which a party has asked to have transmitted.[63]

As Sydney Bailey wisely observes, a polarised situation with no direct contact between adversaries is where the mediator is most useful, but where the responsibility is greatest to ensure that what is communicated is accurate and complete, not softened or modified. There is no other check, no independent way for the recipient to interpret or enlarge upon the message transmitted, so the mediator must be especially careful. At a later stage, the opponents may negotiate directly, even if with hostility, and be able to interpret statements in the light of body language, other statements, or ask for further clarification. Although finding the shuttling role useful, politicians are understandably nervous about depending too much on an intermediary to carry their thoughts.

This kind of shuttling back and forth between sides has been a characteristic of most Quaker mediation work. It is the kind of pre-negotiation role which is necessary in a very polarised situation. This has been well documented by Mike Yarrow for the cases of East-West Germany, India-Pakistan and Nigeria-Biafra.[64] Elmore Jackson has described his experience of moving between Israel and Egypt in 1955.[65] The Quaker involvement between the sides during the period leading up to Zimbabwe independence offers another example. More recent examples include Quaker work in the Middle East and in Northern Ireland.

A case where individual Friends were involved with the initiation and implementation of this kind of work, with considerable Quaker input, but under the auspices of a non-Quaker organisation, was the Cyprus Resettlement Project of 1972-74.[66] Paul Hare, a Quaker who was the one person involved in all the teams that went on these missions to Cyprus, has written:

> The Greek and Turkish sides had not communicated directly about the resettlement issue for ten years. We shuttled back and forth across the "Green line" in Nicosia for a year and a half before we were able to bring representatives of the two sides to the same table.[67]

Shuttle mediation is a broad concept that includes many different aspects of the mediator's role. In the course of going back and forth among the "sides", she may be clarifying misunderstandings, asking innocent questions, interpreting fears, testing possibilities, as well as listening and empathising with each side. In one sense, she is trying to understand each person and his situation well enough to be able to somehow communicate the reality of that person to his opponents. N. Ramamurthy describes how he tries to carry the reality of suffering from one side to another in Sri Lanka.

> When we visited the north this time, it was the first time I flew there; otherwise I use the same route, in a sense [that most people there have to use]. They go by bicycle; I go by truck. They went walking in some areas; I went walking. They went by boat; I went by boat. At least I can see what kind of suffering they are going through.

When they asked me once: "Why are you taking this much trouble to come like this?" I said: "Look, unless I come and see the kind of suffering you have got, I can't go back and say [to other Sri Lankans and to those outside] how you are suffering."

Thése people are going through this much struggle, and we need to ask what motivates them to go on enduring this suffering? If they are able to endure this suffering, what must have gone wrong, what is it that they found so hard to endure before? The hardship they are enduring now seems very much more to me than what they endured before, but they don't want to get back to that situation. So what must have done this? I don't have to give an answer to these people [their opponents, to whom I am describing their suffering], but I can point this out, and say: "Why don't we think about this?"[68]

So the shuttling role is much more than just carrying questions and responses between people. It also means the carrying back and forth of people's experiences — experiences of suffering and hardship, experiences of joy and hope, experiences of doubt and fear, experiences of trying to make some sense of their own situations. The mediator tries to bring to each person some responses to the questions that he has about his opponents; these responses are based on relationships and understanding that have been built up over time. Ultimately, the questions will need to be asked directly: but, for now, indirect communication is a possible option, and the mediator attempts to carry out this role with sensitivity for the feelings and experiences of each side.

Work with texts

In a number of conflict situations, Quakers have decided that their role is to shuttle back and forth among the various parties with a text that sets out the positions of the different sides and then later to publish this text. This was a task undertaken by the "Quaker Mission to the Two Germanies" in September 1963. The resulting report, Journey Through a Wall,[69] was "designed to influence American public opinion and thereby American policy."[70] Roland Warren, who was the Quaker International Affairs Representative (QIAR) in Berlin at the time, has described a problem that emerged with the publication of this report, which had nothing to do with the content of the text:

Inadvertently, a map of the two Germanies inserted by the Philadelphia office without review by the German QIAR was one of the widely-circulating maps which implied ultimate German sovereignty over the territories ceded to the Soviet Union and to Poland after World War II. This caused a flurry of understandable indignation on the part of the East German Peace Council, which had helped organise the visit [by the Quaker delegation], and on the part of the Polish Government.[71]

This example illustrates the importance of taking extreme care before publishing anything related to the situation where Quakers are trying to fill a mediating role.

Another example of this kind of role is the AFSC project of carrying numerous drafts of a text between the sides in the Middle East, which resulted in the publication of <u>Search for Peace in the Middle East</u>.[72] Landrum Bolling has reflected on this experience:

> We wanted to see if it was possible for us to develop a paper that would reflect accurately, objectively and nonemotionally the viewpoints of the parties involved. We set for ourselves the task of trying to be communicators, not mediators, and we constantly had to fight against the accusation that we were trying to be mediators in this conflict. [...] This activity was a very haphazard kind of Quaker amateur happening. It is not social science, but it has been an experience for those of us who participated in it that certainly has added to our knowledge of the area and of the problems, and has given us a deeper understanding of the emotions that lie behind the policies.[73]

Landrum Bolling defines a role of communicator which stops short of mediation. But, for most mediators, communication seems to be one of the roles that a mediator fills in listening to all sides and carrying perceptions, ideas and proposals between the sides.

Texts can be a useful way of working toward an agreed statement, at least of the problem, if not of the solution. As such, they can assist people from the different sides in articulating their own experience more clearly and in ways that can be better understood by others, as well as in appreciating the situation of those from the other side. There can be problems, however, particularly if the text is published as though it were a position statement.

> When the [Quaker] organisation allows its stance to be published, even if it's the 18th draft and has been a useful vehicle for discussion, there is no 19th, but the comparing of all future words and actions with this fixed statement.[74]

What mediators and opponents are learning from trying to agree a text may be jeopardised when something concrete, that is, something set and fixed forever, eventually appears in print. The dynamic is lost, and the capacity for change, as well as the necessary juggling of paradoxical and contradictory experiences and views. Still, one cannot go on forever taking new drafts of a text back and forth for discussion; eventually, people will expect a statement or report to appear.

<u>Work on one side: for internal unity</u>
In these deeply divided societies, there is often an appearance of complete polarisation: that everyone belongs to one of two sides. In fact, the situation is rarely so neat. There are often more than two sides, and fragmentation within the sides. This can make progress toward understanding and negotiations difficult, because each side mistrusts its own splinter groups at least as much as it mistrusts its opponents. An unofficial mediator may devote much of her effort to working with each of the broader sides, separately, to prepare them to move toward direct negotiations.

The pre-negotiating process, I think, can involve, even in the narrowest sense, a mediating between parties, and, in that slightly broader sense, engaging in building constituencies for a negotiating process and in building a knowledge base for the negotiating process.[75]

The role of the mediator, then, may include working on communication within the sides, between factions or groupings, so that they can reach a point where they are willing to designate spokespeople to meet with the other side.

And there may be pressure on the intermediary from factions, as from the larger groupings in the conflict, to agree with one faction rather than working between them.

> Anne Grace: In the [Occupied] Territories, I tend to deal on a visible level with spokespeople of the various factions, as opposed to dealing with the people who may be the actual leaders of those factions. [...] I tease some of the kids, the "shabab", I say: "Maybe you have to make the choice, have to belong to one of the factions, but I don't: I like all of you." But I think the first coordination that was institutionalised among the factions was a result of my efforts. I worked very long and hard on that.
>
> Sue Williams: Your involvement in that, is that based on a sense that it's the right thing to do, that it's important to the process, that it's necessary for political reasons? [...]
>
> Anne: A belief that they'll never get anywhere while they're undercutting each other.
>
> Sue: So it has to do with effectiveness?
>
> Anne: There is a concept of national assets, national unity, that the people deserve, and that they [the leaders of the factions] represent the "leadership" of various political strata within the nation, and they have an obligation to the people, most of whom are not politicised, to represent the nation as a whole.
>
> Sue: [...] You see that clearly as being advantageous to Palestinians. Is there a sense in which that is advantageous to other people in the region, or [...] have you weighed whose interests you are favouring? Is it part of the process that it needs to be that way? Where do other people fit into that scheme?
>
> Anne: Historically, Palestinians have been used and abused by everybody...Arabs or Israelis. And I think that, if you are looking for peaceful solutions in the region, then Palestinians need to have a consensus as opposed to divisiveness.[76]

This is delicate work, because "balanced partiality"[77] is more difficult to maintain while working to strengthen one side. Such concentration on one set of views may appear unbalanced, and may indeed feel so. The mediator may be tempted to become partisan, to believe that internal unity and confidence within this group is essential to a settlement, and thus unconsciously to favour this viewpoint. Remaining in the middle will be difficult, if one is busy working on one side.

Work on one side: for empowerment

As in situations where internal unity is needed, in cases where power is clearly uneven, there may need to be long efforts on one side, in this case aimed at empowerment.

This is often true when the protagonists in a struggle or potential struggle are of very unequal power. The strong — the oppressors — see no need for mediation, except perhaps as a propaganda ploy. They are confident that they can crush any opposition. The weak then need help and encouragement to develop their administrative capacity, political will, know-how, and material resources to the point where they can confidently challenge their oppressors — hopefully by means which are without violence.[78]

Quaker organisations often act in this capacity, working to empower the oppressed or marginalised people in a number of situations, but this is not so often done by representatives trying to act in a more balanced capacity. More often, empowerment is a separate piece of work by Friends, sometimes in parallel with mediation, more often preceding it.

There have been occasions, though, when the mediation process itself seemed to require empowering one side, and Quakers have tried to assist. For example, representatives have arranged for paramilitary or guerrilla groups to have consultants with expertise in constitutional law or technical aspects of disarmament, in order to equalise the negotiating status of the sides. This is part of what Everett Mendelsohn referred to in the statement above (see preceding section "Work on one side: for internal unity") as "building a knowledge base for the negotiating process". It is an advantage of small, inconspicuous organisations to be flexible enough to interpret the role of mediator more broadly, and to make discreet arrangements that do not force the more powerful side to admit publicly that the less powerful side needs assistance in order to be equal partners in negotiation.

This kind of work on one side is uncommon, though sometimes necessary, but it must somehow be kept in the perspective of working to bring opponents together to settle the conflict together. In a situation such as South Africa or the former Rhodesia, for example, where a minority group is maintaining a position of power in what is generally perceived as an unjust situation, the Quaker mediator may, in fact, be assisting a process in which power might move from the minority to the majority. But the intention is that this should happen in a manner which depends on the minority negotiating for itself a positive role in the new situation.

Confidant

Sometimes the role of the mediator is almost that of confidant. Under the stresses of life in conflict, politicians (or, indeed, mediators) may be moved to confide deep personal or spiritual concerns. This is a moving moment, and must be met with sympathy, compassion, and humanity, as well as confidentiality. But it is important not to encourage confidences or offer advice that may later be regretted, since this may

48

damage, not only the relationship with the politician, but his capacity to be trusting or vulnerable in other settings. Quaker mediators are not normally appropriate counsellors for politicians, and this is not the basis of the relationship between them.

We spent an afternoon with a politician who had just learned of a massive bombing in his district. All three of us were shocked, and our emotions were close to the surface. We talked in great depth, asking the familiar fundamental questions, struggling with answers. I don't think he realized that, during most of that time, he had his gun in his hand, so vulnerable did he feel to attack. For some months afterward, he was shy with us, and critical of us for not lining up in opposition to the group that did the bombing. Now, the relationship looks like most of ours with politicians, intermittent and friendly, but in this case with a warmth based on deep sharing.[79]

The close relationships that sometimes develop between the mediator and the political leader can put the mediator in a position of some influence with that particular politician. What a mediator is trying to influence is the process of politics, and the ways politicians relate to each other. In order to do that, she must be careful to maintain a balance of relationships on all sides. She will then be in a position to encourage creative thinking on each side, helping the politicians to speculate about possible options and assuring them that someone on the other side is doing the same.

Being asked for advice

In building close relationships with politicians, mediators often find themselves asking questions about motives, consequences, and possibilities. This offers the political figure the opportunity to try out new ideas, and to speculate about possibilities. But it may also confront him with deeper dilemmas, of the sort that all of us try not to think about too much. In posing such questions, mediators may find themselves being questioned in turn.

People say: "What shall we do?" — that kind of thing. Not very often, but occasionally there will be somebody, and often at the very highest level. You drop this enigma on them: "What are you going to do?", and then their mouth flutters for a moment or two, and then they say: "Do you have any suggestions?"[80]

Mediators generally are wary of offering advice. They report being willing to discuss dilemmas, commiserate, support, encourage, but most avoid outright suggestions. Mediators do not study the conflict with the aim of maximising the benefits and minimising the loss to one side, and their forte is not as strategists. They may offer some examples from their experience of how people in other conflict situations have tried to overcome a particular block, but in such a way that the politician, not the mediator, can decide what might be appropriate in his own situation.

There seem, however, to be no rules of conduct which apply to all the Quaker mediation initiatives studied here. In the work of Quaker International Affairs Representatives [QIARs] between the two Germanies, for example, which covered the years 1962-73, one representative reports that offering his judgment and advice was a significant part of the role.

> The QIARs [representatives] frequently gave their own personal assessment of the situation when requested, and in some cases even made proposals and advocated specific measures.[81]
>
> It appeared that the officials were interested not only in an account of how their actions were perceived on the other side, but also in the assessment of the situation given by the QIARs, who were perceived to be friendly rather than hostile, knowledgeable, and, yes, judgmental (with appropriate tact and discretion).[82]

All mediators report having been asked for their own suggestions. This can be part of a process of encouraging creativity, in which the mediator may suggest examples of ideas which have worked elsewhere, and politicians may use some aspect from this to create a new possibility in their own situation. In one case, the Quakers offered, not their own advice, but the cost of bringing in an outside "expert" for advice on constitutional options.

> The other day someone came to me and said that we must write up a proposal of a federal constitution and pass it on to these [other] people to do it. And I said, "Look. What we can do is what we have already offered to [another group]: If you need a constitutional expert who is not aligned to any side and whom you can consult for an independent opinion, then we will help you to find an international constitutional expert. You will have to tell him what you want and he will make a proposal and you will have to accept that proposal. It will not be a proposal from us, but we will foot the bill."[83]

It is sometimes the case that offering advice may actually mean that the mediator is pointing out something that was written by one of the sides and suggesting this as a way forward.

> Sometimes what has happened is this. They [...] got bogged down in various items. And I said, "Why don't you try this out? Would this not be a way out? You have to find a way. That [solution] is not acceptable to them. This may be a way out, because many solutions have been brought out, by them or thee." [...] I quoted from a paper that [the other side] had written, and I said, "Do you see in that particular paper, they have said this? Is that not a way for getting over this [particular issue]?" And they said, "Yes, there is something in what you say."[84]

It is generally the practice of Quaker mediators, however, to avoid advising particular actions, ideas, or strategies. Adam Curle offers a story, from which identifiers have been removed, to show the difficulties involved in appearing to offer advice or promote solutions.

> On the plane going home, I wrote a letter to [the politician] saying that I thought the war would go on indefinitely to the ruin of everybody, I didn't see any sign of a settlement, unless there was an agreement [to try one possibility, X.] It didn't seem to me that this was all that difficult. He wrote back to me, furious, and he said that "absolutely, positively, if you think that, I don't see any point in our further communication". So I wrote back and said: "I'm terribly sorry, I just sort of tossed it off, off the top of my head"... So, anyway, he forgave me and sent me a Christmas card. A year or so later, I was talking to him, and he said: "You know, we've just come to a very important conclusion. We've decided that, really, the future lies in [possibility X.]"
> I think there's a double reason it's bad [offering advice]. One, it's stepping out of one's role. And the other is that it's very difficult to make any suggestion about what people should do, without appearing to be losing one's impartiality.[85]

This politician did not seem even to remember having been furious at the mention of this idea a year earlier, nor to connect it with Adam Curle as mediator. He eventually adopted the idea enthusiastically. Someone else who is familiar with this example has suggested that the politician was more upset by a comparison of his situation to a particular conflict situation in another country than by the actual possibility suggested to him. In any case, this suggestion, offered at the wrong time or phrased in the wrong way, was nearly enough to ruin the relationship altogether.

Although Quaker mediators generally agree that one ought to be wary of offering advice, still, there are no rigid rules in this kind of work. In some settings, Quaker representatives have been party to relationships where their advice or judgment was often sought, and they have served in rather the capacity of advisor, on one or more sides. This may have been because their assessment of the situation was that direct meetings between the sides were impossible; instead, this was a stage where work needed to be done on each side separately, and dialogue established between mediator and political leader, rather than between opposing leaders.

Roles: What the mediator is not

In addition to describing some of the roles filled by Quaker mediators, it is perhaps useful to point out some of the roles that they tend to **avoid** in doing mediation. Offering advice is one questionable area, and there are a few others.

Mediators do not generally lobby. This is what the politician normally expects, when asked to meet with someone he does not know. He expects pressure to select one of the various options open to him on some issue of the day. It takes time, careful listening, and a demonstrated ability to bring him views he does not usually hear, before he begins to believe that the focus of this kind of mediation is on the process. When the mediator has carefully built this understanding that the role is not lobbying, she may feel undercut if her organisation proceeds to send letters or delegations to push this same politician to vote in a particular way. This does not mean that there should not be lobbying, but that care should be taken to distinguish it from mediation work.

Another area of work in which mediators do not generally engage is advocacy. By this, one generally means pleading the cause of a less powerful group by presenting it to a government or other more powerful group, sometimes by individual cases. Some mediators have done this kind of work at another time, others feel temperamentally or in other ways disinclined to do it. Again, mediators acknowledge that this is important work, and understand that it should be done, even by their own organisation, but it needs to be clearly distinguished from mediation.

> I'm more inclined to move away from advocacy. That's just my nature now, and also my age. It's definitely changed over time. Working with Adam [Curle] has changed, or has reinforced changes in me. I think that advocacy is very important, perhaps the most important; somebody has to speak up, to be heard. But, at the same time, unless we believe that there is a possibility to defeat evil, and good win out totally, and if you don't believe you can do that with arms, I'm not sure you can believe that you can do that with other things, either. You've got to learn to work with people, first of all to recognise that they aren't all evil... I think I'm more comfortable now with what is really a compromising role, in relating to people that were not necessarily nice people, or not doing nice things. That's part of my work.[86]

Joel McClellan has referred to temperament and to life-stage as reasons for emphasising conciliatory rather than confrontational approaches. His concluding remark is important as well: part of the professionalism of being a Quaker Representative is recognising that one's role, in this place and time, means acting in one way rather than another. The organisation may need to ensure that it balances reconciliation with advocacy, peace with justice, mediation with human rights. But the experience of mediators is that they cannot themselves live out all of these roles at once. The balance they seek is the caring relationship with all sides of a conflict, but they do not expect to be able to do this while taking public stances that confront any of the sides or reject them as evil.

Do you ever decide you must say no?

At a mediation training seminar in Moscow, one participant asked: Would you ever refuse to continue as mediator in a situation? Is there a settlement you would not help to negotiate?

My answer was: Yes. I would not be party to an agreement which was unjust, or which resolved one conflict by doing harm to another party who was not present. This does come up in dealing with wars and situations of violence. Although I would generally agree to try to arrange meetings for opponents to talk about almost anything, there are limits to what I would do. Military groups may want to meet together to exchange technical information on weapons, for instance, more efficient ways of killing; I would not be party to that. Political parties might want to discuss ways of marginalising other parties, but I would not convene that discussion. Opposing groups of paramilitaries in Northern Ireland once wanted to talk about negotiating a truce, stating that they would no longer kill each other. Since the effect was that they would continue to kill the rest of us, but in more safety, that seemed to me unjust and unacceptable.[87]

Mediators may find themselves working out all kinds of arrangements between all sorts of parties. It is sometimes difficult to know when the participants are being creative and thinking laterally, and when they are being unfair or scape-goating someone else. Given the premise that participants in a conflict must decide what is an acceptable settlement, most mediators try to withhold their judgment on the content of an agreement.

There are times, however, when a line must be drawn, and it is important to keep this possibility in mind. If a government asks the mediator to arrange for the rebel group to surrender, she must ascertain whether this is the wish of the rebels, and whether it seems to her a just settlement. In the case of the Nigeria–Biafra war, Adam Curle has described how the result of a one-sided victory was unexpectedly positive.[88] In another case, the mediator might feel bound to withdraw. This is one reason that it is so important to be knowledgeable about the nuances of the situation, so that one can understand what is being discussed and see its consequences for all sides.

Although generally willing to accept settlements agreed at fairly by disputants, mediators are also moral beings, and their consciences must be satisfied that the work they are doing is to a good end. Maintaining a position of neutrality in the face of serious injustice or brutality by one side against the other, or against a third party not present, is not appropriate for a Quaker mediator, who does in fact represent certain spiritual as well as moral values.

CHAPTER 8

Qualifications and Qualities of a Mediator

WHAT ARE SOME OF THE QUALITIES and qualifications that make a particular person a good mediator? It has been suggested that some people are just natural mediators, while others would insist that one can learn to be a mediator. Whether they come naturally or are learned, some characteristics seem to be more useful than others in doing mediation.

Willingness to listen to all sides

A mediator, as a person who is in the middle listening to all sides in a conflict, must be someone with a tolerance for quite a wide range of viewpoints. Some people react very negatively, for example, to the suggestion of listening to someone who represents a viewpoint which is very far from their own in terms of right-left politics. Others may abhor the thought of talking with someone who is a member of what society may call a "terrorist" organisation, or someone who commands an army. Experience and conscious learning may extend a natural tolerance, but some personality characteristics seem to preclude acting as mediator. A dogmatic or ideologically rigid individual would be unlikely by nature to listen sympathetically to the variety of strongly-held positions that could be involved in a particular political conflict. Such a person might do well in other activities, such as advocacy, which are in no way inferior to mediation, but simply different.

Belief systems keep people apart, mediators as well as opponents. Dealing with people one knows have caused death may be particularly difficult for a pacifist. Similarly, it may seem unconscionable to talk civilly with leaders of governments which behave oppressively, because this behaviour violates basic values of justice. Yet, if the conflict is ever to be resolved, the mediator sees the need to be able to hear all these people, and help them to begin to hear each other. After all, they have suffered more than she has, and are at greater risk.

> When I said to one of the people that I deal with in Northern Ireland, "Why don't you talk about this with a person on the other side?" he said, "I couldn't do that." I said, "Why not? You're doing it with me." He responded, "Yes, but you don't want to kill me."[89]

54

This man will probably, one day, have to sit across the table from someone who has tried to kill him, and calmly sip his tea and argue about article two of the constitution and the boundaries of voting districts. The mediator listens, in order to help him to listen.

Listening is not a purely neutral and passive act. One aspect of listening is that it permits, even obliges, the other person to set his thoughts in order, and look at the causes and consequences of his actions. The following story shows the leader of a guerrilla army explaining an atrocity.

> Joe Elder: We felt it was important to let them be aware that we knew they were bullies. [...] For example, after they massacred a bunch of people [in another grouping on their own side.] These were people they'd been working with, and they kind of picked the day, and they killed between 100 and 200 of them. [...]
>
> So, the next time we met [...] Adam [Curle] said: "You know, we are puzzled. First of all, is it true? And could you explain it, because to us, as Quakers, it's very difficult to understand."
>
> And it was very interesting. He [our contact] said: "Revolutions go through certain stages, and you have to see what stage you are in." - sort of a straight take-off from Castro. "You form a united front with anybody who agrees with you in the armed struggle, until you reach a point when you are beginning to succeed, and then you have to eliminate the opposition. And I have no personal grudges against these folks [in the other grouping], they are nice young men, but in order for this to succeed, at a certain point, we have to eliminate them." And what do you say to that, as a Quaker? [...]
>
> Sue Williams: Well, what did you say as a Quaker, when this chap finished explaining that the logic of the revolution required that they massacre the other side?
>
> Joe: We just said we were opposed to killing in any form, and they understood that from day one. But [...] I thought often it wasn't the messages we were carrying, so much as it was the event itself, and the fact that what we were asking both sides was: "What would it take to stop the fighting?" And it was clear that, often, they hadn't thought about that, because the war was just such a basic thing. And sometimes you felt that they were just making it up as they went along.[90]

One may hear such chilling stories, and have great difficulty in continuing to relate to the story-teller on any level. The mediator sometimes has the feeling Joe Elder describes, of holding these people to account, of reminding them that there is something beyond the exigencies of war by which to judge actions. But the mediator does not judge the person, or refuse further contact with him. This is partly because she recognises the capacity for evil, the shadow side of each person, as well as the capacity for good.

One important, perhaps unexpected quality of a mediator is precisely this awareness of her own shadow side, the realisation that each of us is capable of evil as well as good, and that even the most awful action cannot be dismissed as monstrous or inhuman: it is all too human. Someone too naive, too fragile, or too good, may be over-whelmed by the cold, calculating strategies that devalue life. In order to be useful in this kind of situation, the mediator will need to acknowledge these blocks, but then go through them, and emerge with a still greater determination to uphold the value of life and the individual's capacity for good as well as evil.

Confidentiality and discretion

Another characteristic that many practitioners believe is important to the medi-ating role is the ability to keep information confidential when the situation requires it. Along with this, the ability to work behind the scene without the need for recognition and publicity has been identified as very important by a number of Quaker mediators. "It's almost impossible to develop relationships of trust in the blaze of publicity."[91] In many situations, it seems that the parties are willing to use a mediator for communica-tion with the other side precisely because there is an expectation of confidentiality.

A Northern Ireland politician, who had asked the Quaker House representa-tives to carry a verbal message to another political leader, later acknowledged that he had offers from others willing to fill this role. However, he said that he preferred to use Quakers because "you don't seem to have a vested interest in any one side here, but you do have contacts in the right places in order to get the message through without any publicity."[92]

Perhaps one significant quality here is having a low-key approach to mediation, and a strong enough ego so that one does not need to claim credit for the work. The parties involved in the mediation must be able to claim credit for any successes, but dis-tance themselves by reporting that the process was unofficial, informal, and without authority, if things seem to go wrong. The fact that there is no public recognition for this role will allow the parties to disclaim any contact with the other side until they are ready to have it known publicly.

Memory, writing and language skills

Good memory, writing abilities and appropriate language proficiency are some other qualifications that are very important for doing mediation. It is essential to the process that the mediator be able to remember the facts of a particular meeting or inter-view. Getting the wording right is very important when one is conveying information, perceptions, fears, ideas or proposals from one party to another. However, most Quaker mediators do not take written notes during meeting, to make it clear that statements made really will not be attributed. On those rare occasions when a politician wants to be sure that the wording is correct, he will suggest that notes be written; otherwise, most mediators reported that they could remember most of what went on, and particularly new or striking wording. These skills are also necessary for writing accurate reports of the mediation activity for internal use, as well as less detailed reports for the supporting organisation.

Being able to speak the languages of the parties in conflict seems an obviously important skill in this kind of delicate work, where words are so important. Language ability can also be a great asset in building trust and confidence. N. Ramamurthy, a Tamil Quaker, describes his experience in Sri Lanka:

> If you translate Tamil into English, it may sound different from what we mean. And also an important thing is that I am speaking to them in Tamil. The majority of these cadres became obsessed with language. Even though they knew English, they were testing me: "You are a Tamil, we will only talk to you in Tamil."
>
> There were seven different Tamil groups. I asked them all to come together. One [...] leader organised a group [...], and they insisted that I should talk in Tamil. He begged me, he said: "These people will not understand English. They insist on you talking in Tamil. You talk to them in Tamil. Where you are not able to do it, branch into English and I will translate it. But you tell them your problem. Don't let me do that." So I spoke to them [in Tamil], and it immediately brought us closer together.[93]

In this case, the mediator speaks the language of one side, but has to depend upon an interpreter for talking with Sinhalese speakers on the other side. Here he describes a meeting with a Buddhist monk:

> Yes, he can speak a certain amount of English. But he likes to speak in Sinhalese. He used to appoint someone to explain to him in Sinhalese. I was speaking in English. This man was translating to him. He was trying to translate what the monk was telling me. And I knew that there are certain Sinhalese words that are similar to Tamil words. Now this guy was giving a wrong translation, and I straightaway said: "I don't think that [he] has mentioned this. [He] has been saying so and so and I think you have interpreted it wrongly." So I said to [the monk]: "This is what you have been saying. Am I right?" And he said: "You are right", in English.[94]

So even a basic understanding of a language can help the mediator to recognise a wrong interpretation. If at all possible, a mediation team should include people who speak, or at least understand, the languages of the groups they will be meeting. The lack of language skills was identified as a problem for a team involved in Cyprus:

> Another fundamental limitation was the lack of Greek or Turkish language speakers. The difference made by having a fluent Turkish speaker in [one location] was very considerable. As a thought for future such actions, a number of project members who speak the indigenous language should be a priority in selection.[95]

Similarly, T.J. Pickvance identified lack of adequate language skills as a problem when he was with a Quaker delegation visiting Italy, Austria, and the disputed territory of South Tyrol.

Immediately we began interviewing we were in difficulties, the extent of which only became apparent later. Languages were the most obvious. [...] A good general knowledge of a language is certainly not adequate for a detailed study of a conflict. Even an excellent knowledge is insufficient if it does not include the political vocabulary in both tongues and also the special terms which spring from the local laws and culture of the linguistic minority.[96]

The vocabulary and special terms that are referred to here can not easily be learned and understood without first-hand experience of the situation and how people use their language. In Northern Ireland, for example, an outsider who speaks fluent English might not realise the significance of the words used to describe the "Anglo-Irish Agreement". The name suggests that it is an agreement between the English and the Irish, ignoring the fact that the majority in Northern Ireland identify themselves as "British", but not "English". If there is any hope of these people identifying with such an agreement, then "British-Irish Agreement" might be a better way of describing it. It would seem that, in addition to speaking the language well, the mediator needs to live with the local usage of the language for some time, in order really to know how people use particular words in that context.

Intuition and other qualities

There are a number of other less tangible qualities - sensitivity to the cultures involved, humility and openness to learn from one's mistakes, patience and perseverance - which have also been identified as necessary for potential mediators. Perhaps one of the least tangible, but most important qualities, is a kind of intuitiveness that allows one to make decisions about whom to contact, to know how to approach them, to judge when the timing is right to pursue contacts, and to respond to the human as well as the divine in the various parties. Joel McClellan described it this way:

Basically, there are two types of detectives in the world, as far as I'm concerned. There is the Hercule Poirot, who carefully reasons everything out. Then there is the Inspector Maigret, who every now and then gets a visitor from the United States who comes to see what his techniques are and how he does it. And he's terribly embarrassed, because he spends most of his time drinking a glass of this and a glass of that with the man, and there is nothing that really happens. One is obviously intuitive and the other is much more rational. There is so much of the work in developing those things that you can't report back, or when you do or try to, it seems so self-serving that you just forget about it. In talking to a super-rational person, I don't know how to explain how I started this rela-tionship.[97]

Intuitiveness is, indeed, often difficult to explain to a more rational person, and the two types of personality can sometimes clash. But it does seem possible to combine intuition with a more rational analysis of the conflict, as described below:

I think I'm intuitive, maybe in a different sense, in that, in looking at a conflict situation and following what's being reported in the newspapers and what people are saying publicly, I can sometimes sense who are the people who are most likely to be accommodating. It's not just ignorant intuition, it's based on observing the situation and then saying "Now seems like the right time to be contacting this person."[98]

Tolerance for ambiguity, transparency and uncertainty

Mediators need to be willing to listen empathetically to all sides, maintaining a tolerance for ambiguity in the relationships that they form. One mediator put it this way:

Too often, in this kind of work, you do have to be able or willing to live with a lot greater kind of ambiguity than you like. Not only the intellectual or substantive ambiguity, but also the ambiguity of the interaction, of whether something is happening in the best way.[99]

The process requires that one hold different, even contradictory, hypotheses at the same time. In this, as in other respects, one aspect of the mediator's task is to model this behaviour, as she will be asking the political or paramilitary people to behave this way. They will need to hold their own views and let contrary views rest beside them, without leaping to resolve the tension by eliminating the contradiction. In the process as well, the paradox is that trust is necessary in order to get even to the point of negotiating with the other side, whom one does not trust. And, as for the opponents, so for the mediator, the results may remain ambiguous: Was the timing right? Should the agenda have included other issues? Would more consultation with the negotiators have helped or hindered? Such questions are unlikely ever to be resolved, and one must simply live with them.

A quality that is related to this tolerance for ambiguity is the ability to become transparent in a relationship. This probably goes hand-in-hand with a strong ego that does not require the satisfaction of being seen as an important person in the relationship. It was described by one of the representatives in Belfast:

As people got to know us, we began to be transparent. I mean, they began to look through us and then see the people they wanted to talk to, instead of us.[100]

The relationship becomes transparent, in this sense, when the parties to it are no longer concentrating on each other, no longer working on their relationship, but working together toward a common purpose. This may be a relatively short-term, functional purpose, such as the setting up of a particular meeting or conference, or it may be much broader, such as the transformation of the political process in their situation from adversarial and hostile to more cooperative. In either case, trust exists sufficiently so that attention may be focused outward rather than inward. At this stage, the political or paramilitary leader may focus on opponents he meets with, taking the mediator for granted.

This can be hard on the ego, and can also leave the mediator unsure whether she is being useful or whether she is being "used", in a negative, manipulative sense. This ambiguity, too, is reported by many mediators, and the ability to tolerate it seems to be a quality needed to do the work.

Still another related issue is the capacity to work in a small way on momentous issues, often unsure of one's footing, and unlikely ever to be sure of one's impact.

> This is an enormous conflict, and there's no way to be able, at any one time and in any one thought, to comprehend all of it. The sheer enormity of it gets to you after a while. When you are dealing with so many bits and pieces, it is hard to get a full handle on it.[101]

Identification with Quaker principles and values

For mediation being done under Quaker auspices, it is important that the mediators be either members of the Religious Society of Friends or at least very familiar and comfortable with Quaker values of nonviolence and listening to that of God in every person. These are values that political leaders seem to recognise and respect in the relationships that they form with Quaker representatives, although, of course, these qualities and values are not exclusive to Quakers.

It is important that the practice of mediation be consistent with the values and principles that we express as a religious body. Quaker representatives are not offering only a technical service, but also a group's concern for victims on all sides and an organisation's willingness to help the parties come together to find nonviolent ways of dealing with the conflict. To lose sight of the spiritual basis of this work can lead one to forget the corporate nature of the role.

One of the principled positions of Quakerism is a kind of pacifism that is also an activism. Pacifism has often been discredited by suggesting that it means one will do nothing in the face of violence; what some call "passivism." The kind of pacifism that Quaker mediators could be expected to believe in and demonstrate in their lives is an abhorrence of violence which leads one to become engaged in the situation of violence in a positive way. Someone who has been associated with Friends work in the Middle East for many years has given a very interesting definition of pacifism:

> I've pushed hard to even insist that the people they hire [as Middle East Representative] be real pacifists, in the true sense of really being able to deal with two parties and not allow themselves to become so committed to one that they disrespect the other.[102]

The pacifism of the mediator, then, is not merely the refusal to bear arms, but the belief that violent conflicts should be worked on, and that their resolution or improvement will come from agreement and change by the parties themselves. This leads the mediator to a determination to respect each side and each viewpoint in the situation, and to a commitment to work toward rebuilding the broken relationships.

<u>What about professionalism?</u>

Professionalism is a concept about which many Quakers have mixed feelings. In relation to the work of mediators, it might suggest a kind of expertise and approach with which some are uncomfortable. Yet, if Friends want to be taken seriously by people who are in positions of political leadership, then the mediators must be able to take themselves seriously in the role which they are offering to these politicians.

> I just felt that we really are amateurs. And, again, there's an up side and a down side to being an amateur. The up side being, that people will often have a kind of confidence in you, because you aren't a career diplomat, your promotion isn't going to depend on your working out some kind of a deal or something. And the negative is that, if you aren't there at that moment when you're supposed to be, you can miss a big opportunity. And things can go wildly off the rails, where, had you been there, you could have perhaps carried a message which might have prevented somebody from saying something.[103]
>
> And I think that what we do that does look professional, even though we are amateurs, is that fact that we do repeat. That we say we're going to come back, and we do come back. That we say it's going to be confidential, and it is confidential. We say that what's off the record is indeed off the record. And, over a period of time, we aren't giving press scoops, we aren't in any way apparently advancing our own careers.[104]

In Joe Elder's terms, amateurism comes from a lack of financial or professional self-interest, and implies an intermittent availability that can be a problem with non-residential, flying-in-and-out patterns of mediation. In other situations, Quaker representatives and mediators are resident, so the coming and going is not an issue, but confidentiality and humility remain. But the amateur status does not mean that an unofficial mediator can be any less serious, well-informed, or critical in doing the work. The parties will judge the mediator according to the role she defines for herself, and they notice promises made and kept.   ·

In this context, a professional could be described as a person who has, through training and experience, developed a range of skills and qualities that make her particularly well-suited to be able to assist a process of communication between parties who are in conflict. A commitment to listening to all sides, without making judgments or taking sides, and a willingness to immerse oneself in the complexity of the political conflict are part of this professionalism. There would be little support for an emphasis on professionalism that was intended to be exclusive, however.

> You want to leave room for the people who aren't coming out of the professions to do it, but you want to develop the skills which allow you to do it in a manner which is fully competent, and has the qualities you'd look for in professional work. You don't want to be exclusionary in a professional form. Leave room for people like us to take part, we're all amateurs.[105]

This entire area of work has been done by individuals who began as amateurs, that is, without credentials in political mediation, indeed, without having identified that as an area of work. They have, however, been people who analysed their experiences, learned consciously from what they and others had done, and tried to pass on some of their learning.

There is a danger that an emphasis on professionalism can lead to a kind of competitiveness between mediators that is not helpful. People who have developed, or have been trained in, particular models of mediation might try to "sell" their services as a package arrangement, without really understanding the local circumstances.

Enshrined in the National Peace Accord (signed in 1991 by many parties in South Africa, including the government, the ANC, and Inkatha) is a section on dispute resolution [which] stipulates the creation of regional and local Dispute Resolution Committees. [...]

Many of the mediators are taking this as an invitation to bid, offering a set programme that could be implemented anywhere, and competing with each other for the contract to set up committees and dispute centres all over the country. [..] The effect seems to be to centralise the process, and encourage slick presentations and programmes that claim to do everything. This, in turn, marginalises precisely those people who are suffering from the conflict. A decentralised process could build on locally-defined problems and solutions, and encourage the development of local people as mediators. Bidding for contracts encourages the importation of models developed elsewhere, and rewards people with experience in using the model, rather than experience in the local situation.[106]

At the same time, there are aspects of mediating in armed conflicts that small teams of Quakers, or other "amateurs", cannot do as well as the United Nations, for example.

What makes us amateurs? We lack the whole political infrastructure of professionals. For example, at one point, the possibility was raised of there being a cease-fire that Quakers might monitor, and I felt it was very unwise. Because, if they violate the cease-fire, what do we do? We're not trained on weapons and all the rest. So we can't offer the kind of service that the UN could offer or a diplomatic service could offer.

And even arranging meetings - which you have done - the fear that one of the sides would use us as a trap and assassinate the other side, and there goes our credibility for decades. So I was very, very reluctant whenever we appeared to be in a position where we were asking people to put their lives on the line, because we couldn't even begin to guarantee their security.[107]

Quaker professionalism has a spiritual component as well. In one sense, the Quaker representative who is doing mediation work is a kind of Quaker missionary. She is carrying out a mission which emerges from Friends' belief that there is "that of God in everyone" and from the long-standing testimony to peace and nonviolence. The spiritual grounding of the approach to mediation, and its corporate testing, give it a kind of professionalism that transcends technical expertise. Quaker mediators can let their lives speak in a way that may look professional because of the disciplined adherence to a role of confidentiality, balanced concern, and self-effacing facilitation.

The person in the middle is expected to behave fairly, as a minimal requirement. But mediators expect much more of themselves: to be able to understand each group's position, to sympathise with each individual's experience, to see how people have ended up where they are, and to glimpse intuitively where they hope to go in the best and most idealistic parts of themselves. This profound feeling of caring about all sides will then manifest itself in behaviour which is impartial, empowering, and self-effacing. The mediators will convey views and set up channels between the sides, and then get out of the way. And all of this is done by supremely ordinary, imperfect human beings, working with other imperfect (though perhaps less ordinary) human beings.

CHAPTER 9

Learning How to Act as Mediator

MEDIATORS LEARN THROUGH BOTH FORMAL training and experience. General training in mediation, suitable for family or community disputes, for example, provides a useful grounding in the approach and some of the processes and techniques that have proven to be useful in particular situations. Political mediation is a special form, and specific models and formats do not seem to transfer well from other kinds of mediation or from one cultural situation to another. Still, many mediators have found the all-purpose training to be a useful basis on which to build.

Listening skills are something that one can and should be trained for when preparing to take on a mediating role. Many courses in counselling or conflict resolution include training in how to actively listen to people's feelings and positions.

Tolerance and empathy for all sides are more difficult to learn by training. Perhaps these are qualities that one must have inherently, or that one nurtures through long experience of living and working with people from very diverse backgrounds and viewpoints.

Learning through life experience

Mediators themselves commonly cite life experience as a crucial factor in their own learning, and particularly the experience of living in situations of violent conflict. It is not a matter of cavalierly exposing someone to danger, but of discovering that people do live in places that seem uninhabitable on our television screens, in Beirut and Belfast, Mogadishu and Nagorno-Karabakh. All of us have much to learn from people who continue to work for peace in the midst of war, and much to learn about ourselves.

> If one did want to set up a training programme, it would be very interesting to have both the academic stuff, the theoretical stuff, and then these kinds of experiences, where you are living in places where the death squads are operating and people's lives are at risk, and you are in the middle of this, too, and have to learn to deal with your own feelings and your own temporality.[108]

When one of the parties in conflict is describing his experience of being at war with another side, and of having had family members or close friends killed, the mediator will be more able to understand the feelings that are being described, if she has had something of this kind of experience herself. Even for those not engaged as mediators, to try to do something about a situation of violence, without understanding the risks, may mean unwittingly exposing others to greater risk. One Quaker representative describes a conference organised in a "safe" country, where participants were coming from violent conflicts.

> Before people went, there was a draft agenda that was sent out, and it had somebody from here on a panel, and people hadn't checked it out. So I sent a fax, and said: "Never show anybody's name appearing on anything until you ask them, because of the situation here. People have got killed." [...]
> It was the organisers, who were dealing with areas of conflict, but not having the experience of **being** in an area of conflict. And when I got there, they were actually taping sessions![109]

There is a certain kind of solidarity and sensitivity that comes from having been touched personally by violence, and this cannot be learned in a training course.

In the midst of violence, mediators are usually aware that they have the luxury of being able to move around without worrying too much, because they are not known and are not particularly targeted. Occasionally (though rarely, in the experience of those consulted here), mediators may not only be subject to the "normal" level of risk, but be singled out for threats and violence. Joe Elder describes his feelings in such a situation, when anyone trying to promote peaceful solutions was under threat:

> It was different. We were threatened. In the abstract. Because people were getting these notices: "If you haven't left in two weeks, we cannot be responsible for your survival", something like that. And then, you have your family, and the people you're meeting with. It was just a different ballgame there for a while.[110]

Intermediaries were targeted because of their role, because they moved between the sides, and suddenly they had to cope with feelings and questions which seemed much more urgent because they affected the mediator's personal life, family, and contacts. This is actually much closer to what political and paramilitary leaders live with all the time. It is educational for mediators to have to face the reality of death threats, rather than always being coolly removed and dismissive of threats which actually affect others.

When a mediator is asking parties to take the risk of meeting someone from the other side, she has to have some understanding of what the consequences could be for this person. He could be labelled a traitor by his own side and be ostracised or killed for that reason. He could be set up by the other side for assassination, if they know where and when he is to be meeting. A mediator with experience of living unarmed in a war will better understand what it means to an armed group to lay down their arms and agree to a cease-fire. These are not concerns that can be taken lightly, and the mediator with experience of violent conflict may be more sensitive to the choices the other person is faced with, better able to help that person assess the risks and find the source of courage, and more likely to understand and acknowledge positive aspects of actions.

<u>Learning about the particular situation</u>
Acquiring a thorough knowledge of the situation and of the positions of all the sides is something that must be a high priority for any mediator in preparing for this role. She may already have some understanding of the political situation through previous involvement or study, but what is required here is a willingness to become totally immersed in the complexity and the detail that people are likely to discuss. Mike Yarrow described it this way:

One cannot overemphasize the importance of knowledge and intelligent appraisal of the issues at stake, the factions involved, the background history, the sensitive points, the stated and the likely non-negotiable items, the elements of the conflict that may be alleviated, and so on. This kind of expertise makes all the difference between the well-intentioned bungler and the helpful mediator. All this proficiency does not have to be the endowment of one person of the team, but the resources need to be available. This is the point at which historians and conflict analysts should be available to the practitioners, and the practitioners should know when they need such help.[111]

Beyond being well-informed in a factual sense, the mediator will need to live with the situation to the point of being able to see and feel how people caught up in it perceive events. This means being empathetically aware of how various people feel in response to the same incident, and being able to convey the whole range of feelings and experiences around the broken circle of communication.

The forming of teams will be dealt with later, but it is worth noting here that one person does not have to hold all the knowledge and expertise. Yet it is important that each individual Quaker take this aspect very seriously in preparing herself to be a mediator. One piece of research, in the arena of general negotiation rather than politics, seems to indicate that the expertise or "perceived ability" of the mediator is more important than impartiality in terms of the impact on the outcome of negotiations.[112]

<u>Learning "on the job"</u>
Often, new team members serve a kind of apprenticeship, by accompanying an experienced mediator and slowly trying their hand. This also offers the opportunity to learn by a "case study" method, analysing each meeting and activity, and discussing what did and did not happen, what choices and decisions were made on the spot, and what can be done next. One difficulty has been the limited number of people with real experience of mediation, and apprenticeships or expanded teams may be one way to meet this need.

Experienced mediators also learn as they go. Indeed, this seems to be the major way that this kind of work is learned. People bring to it a variety of skills and experiences, and use these to analyse meetings and statements, and to make decisions about how to proceed. A number of mediators have mentioned that they have a kind of intuitive sense of what's possible in a situation, and that this comes from having more experience of the particular situation, and more experience in a variety of settings.

Sydney Bailey, in discussing a short-term mediation effort in the Middle East, says:

> We made mistakes then, and I've learnt from my own mistakes: what I haven't learnt from is other people's, yet. [...] I think we need some case studies of Quaker mediation. We've got about six published accounts[113] now, and one unpublished one.[114]

One difficulty with learning by discussion of cases has been the necessary confidentiality of the material. There seem to be, at the time of writing, considerable interest in mediation, a number of writing and documentation projects concerned with mediation, and a rapidly expanding number of people offering to act as mediators in different settings. Without focusing too exclusively on credentials, it would be useful to find new and acceptably confidential ways of ensuring that new people benefit as much as possible from others' experience, and are suitably supervised and supported in their efforts.

CHAPTER 10

Forming a Mediation Team

As a general rule, most mediators agree that it is dangerous to the process as well as to the mediator for an individual to undertake a mediating role alone, though individuals have nonetheless sometimes been led to act alone when necessary.

Difficulties in undertaking work alone

Mediators have found it very important to have others to share the work, people who notice different things, someone to bounce ideas around with, and someone to celebrate or commiserate with.

> I've never really done a big thing by myself. I never started one, but I have been by myself to both Sri Lanka and to Nigeria, and also in Zimbabwe. I found it rather difficult, really. I didn't like it. It's a big responsibility. One gets tired, one gets worried. One wants to discuss it with somebody else and say: "What did that guy really mean when he said that?" [...] and: "What do we do next?"[115]

As with the belief in collective testing, there is a general preference for tempering one person's enthusiasm or dismay by the presence of a second observer, and by the oversight of a group.

However, individuals have sometimes felt called to proceed alone, and this may be necessary. Even those who do normally work alone may appreciate, when possible, the support of other individual Friends and opportunities for collective guidance. H W van der Merwe, who works in South Africa, sometimes under the auspices of the Centre for Intergroup Studies, and sometimes alone, has expressed appreciation for having other Quakers visiting to work with him and Quaker support committees meeting to uphold him.[116] For such a person, being accompanied by other Quaker mediators with experience in different conflict situations can increase his credibility, by making it clear that the Society of Friends does have some kind of collective experience and concern which transcends one individual, however talented, in one place and time.

Combinations

Perhaps the ideal situation is to form teams of mediators who combine a variety of the required qualities. Someone with exceptional listening and interpersonal skills might work with a person who has had experience of living and working in the particular conflict situation and knows the language of at least one side. A third person might bring strengths in organisational skills and writing abilities.

The nature of this work requires the mediators to be well-organised, flexible enough to accept sudden changes in plan or in events, and able to be genuinely interested in meeting a great variety of people, based on different kinds of relationships and approaches. Team members may be selected originally for a variety of skills and experiences, but all must commit themselves to a long-term process of coming to know the situation and the parties. Whatever their initial expertise, they must also become experts in the conflict.

Perhaps most importantly, the team members must be able work together under sometimes difficult and stressful circumstances. The sorts of people who have the initiative, persistence, and self-confidence to set off to sort out wars do not seem likely to make good members of teams: it reminds one of the joke about herding kangaroos. There are some who finally prefer to work alone, others whose circumstances make them work alone, but many have become members of teams.

Teamwork can be quite difficult when one or more of the team members becomes too dominant in the process. It is important that all team members be involved in decisions about how to proceed with the initiative. Communication between the various team members has sometimes been a problem when they are coming from different countries and continents and are visiting the area concerned at different times. The sponsoring organisation needs to ensure that all team members are kept informed and involved in the process at each stage.

There are, of course, mixed reports on these teams, but many seem to have kept their sights on divine inspiration and the greatness of the enterprise, and achieved a remarkable degree of teamwork. The Quaker team in the India–Pakistan situation in 1966 seems a good illustration of this quality of teamwork:

There is unanimous testimony from the team members and observers that there was no sense of rivalry or jealousy in their relations, no jockeying for position in the interviews, no pride of paternity in an idea or a phrase, and no post-mortem criticisms. This harmony of teamwork arose largely from a common dedication to an important job and from a sense of the group's strong support in the two home committees. It is also clear that none of the three required large ego satisfaction from the exercise. They did not have a future reputation at stake, a book to write, and an individual hypothesis to prove.[117]

Often the teams in residential posts have been married couples appointed to work together in this role. The couples need a strong relationship if they are going to be asked to undertake work which can be quite stressful and unpredictable in its scope and intensity. The couples have sometimes chosen to divide the work in some way, but they need to consult together regularly, particularly if they are each working primarily with different parties to the conflict.

Balancing the teams

When teams are being gathered to undertake mediation, the balance of people in terms of age, sex and nationality is a factor to be considered. Sydney Bailey, who is British, regarded it as helpful to be teamed in one case with an American:

In the '73 case [in the Middle East], there was a great advantage in Paul Johnson and I working together, because then it didn't seem as if it was the foreign policy of a particular government.[118]

By and large, Quaker mediators in the past have been men in their middle years or older, most of them either British or American. The situations where couples have worked together have obviously included both sexes, but the mediation teams that go out on short-term missions are often made up of only men. Some say that men are more acceptable in this role of dealing with political leaders and armed groups, but recent experience in both Northern Ireland and in the Middle East seems to have disproved this notion. The female member of the married couple in both situations has been able to develop good working relationships with senior politicians and leaders of armed groups.

The matter of age has been a more difficult one, in that very young people have not so easily engaged with politicians, perhaps not surprisingly. Their youth and lack of life experience seems to make it difficult for them to be taken seriously in the role of mediating between political figures. In many cultures, older people are treated with great deference, and this can be an asset, though it may also lead to expectations that the mediator will offer advice or solve problems. Perceptions of higher class or caste may also produce more deferential attitudes, though this is complex when the mediator is an outsider who does not have an agreed status, and the perceptions become less predictable.

Insiders or Outsiders?

The nationality of the mediators does not seem to be a crucial factor in determining their acceptability. The work in Northern Ireland has been done by Northern Irish, English and American Quakers. In each case, they have been tested before they would be trusted by the politicians, but the fact that they were Quakers, who are a respected group in that situation, seemed to be more important than their nationality. The work of Joan and Billy Sinton in Northern Ireland and of H W van der Merwe in South Africa has shown that Quakers can be accepted as unbiased third parties in their own country, although this does not come without hard work.

The experience of a Tamil Quaker involved in Sri Lanka illustrates the fact that being from the region concerned can be an asset. He describes how he got involved with mediation after two years of staying in the background and letting the "outsiders" form the mediation team.

The first two years I said I must avoid any kind of suspicion because I am a Tamil. So I made a point of being behind, in the background, providing any kind of help to these people, but sending [...] others who are non-Indian, non-local, clearly outsiders, and who are Quakers. It is important to build the confidence from the government side that there is complete neutrality, and that helped. Of course, when [the others] went, they told their contacts that I am a Quaker, I am a Tamil, and I am doing a lot of work maintaining contacts, and they should meet me sometime. And one in particular said: "That's fine, but let him not come now. I will meet him when I come to London." So two years later he came to London and we had a meeting. And at that time he was interviewing me, and I told him the reasons why I didn't go. I said: "I don't want anybody to go back and say you are selling Sri Lanka to a Tamil. That kind of talk will come, and that's why I am not coming." And he said to me: "You are from our part of the world, you know the cultural sensitivities, it would be good if you did come, and go and meet with them yourself." And, so, that's when I began to go there.[119]

In another sense, local people, with a deep understanding of local experiences and feelings, and a commitment to work in their own situation, may be trusted **because** they are local. When outsiders come bringing apparent impartiality, they must work to demonstrate that they actually care about the situation, and are connected to the parties. Perhaps insiders, whose concern and connections are apparent, do parallel work in demonstrating an ability to behave impartially. Certainly, ignorance is no asset. And, as is indicated in the work of John Paul Lederach, a Mennonite working in Central America, the best teams might be composed of insiders as well as outsiders.[120]

Not to include local people smacks of neo-colonialism, as well as great arrogance in presuming that an outsider's ignorance is preferable to an insider's knowledge. And, by definition, outsiders leave, taking their learning and contacts with them, while insiders remain. In recent years, there has perhaps been a greater willingness to look at possibilities of working together with local people, not only learning from them, but including them directly in mediation teams. Uganda is one situation where Quakers worked in a supportive capacity, while local people were the visible mediators. In Sri Lanka and in Northern Ireland, Quaker representatives made some efforts to provide training for local people using cases and examples offered by the local situation. But it is important to remember that local people may be more vulnerable to attack by any of the sides; while they can themselves choose to undertake a dangerous role, their special vulnerability must be kept in mind.

CHAPTER 11

Organisational Responsibilities

MEDIATION INITIATIVES THAT ARE UNDERTAKEN under the auspices of a Quaker organisation will place certain responsibilities and demands on the organisation. These responsibilities include:

— deciding whether and when to become involved,
— setting objectives and priorities for the work,
— allocating the resources to undertake and sustain the
    initiative in a professional way,
— finding the people to form the mediation team,
— facilitating communication between different initiatives,
— making links with other Quaker work, as appropriate,
— being aware of mediation efforts undertaken by other
    organisations, and making contacts as necessary,
— providing for on-going administration and assessment, and
— making decisions about when to bring the project to an end.

The demands on the organisation may be unpredictable, since the need for travel funds, personnel, and other resources will depend on the changing situation. The usefulness of Quaker mediators will depend on their long-term commitment to the situation, as well as the trust and credibility that they are able to establish, and the relative positions of the various parties as the situation changes.

Criteria for involvement

There are many factors or criteria that should be assessed in deciding whether to become involved. What is the previous involvement or experience of Quakers in the region? A suggestion about the possibility of mediation might arise from a situation where Friends are already involved in some other way. Northern Irish Friends had been doing humanitarian work with victims of sectarian violence, as well as offering services for visitors to prisoners on both sides, before any Quakers became involved in facilitating communication between the political groups. In Southern Rhodesia (now Zimbabwe), Friends had been involved in establishing a Rural Training Centre, and have had development workers and international affairs representatives working in the country since the late 1950s. In the Middle East, the Friends Schools in Ramallah had educated many young Palestinians over the years, and Friends had worked extensively with

72

Jewish refugees in Europe, and Palestinian refugees in Gaza and elsewhere. All of these activities lend credibility to the notion that Quakers are concerned about victims in conflict situations.

But there are many other factors that must be examined before taking a decision to become involved:

— Is the situation at a stalemate that would benefit from the kind of slow, quiet diplomacy that Friends have to offer?

— Are any of the key players in the conflict known to Friends, or is it possible that Quakers could get to know them, perhaps through people who have previously participated in conferences for diplomats or in Quaker work at the UN?

— Can the organisation find the people and funds to sustain the initiative for as long as necessary, if relationships of trust are able to be established and are useful in facilitating communication between the sides?

These are some of the questions which should be asked by the Quaker body which is considering mediation work. The final decision, of course, is made in a spiritual process of discernment, seeking divine leadings and a clear sense that it is right to attempt to assist in this situation. Committees will take into account a great many factors, but reason is not necessarily the final criterion. As Adam Curle said about one situation, "This may not be where we would have thought of working, but sometimes the situation chooses us, and we must be open to it."[121]

Setting of priorities and objectives

Having made a decision to become involved, the setting of priorities and objectives would be the next step. It is not always possible to have clearly defined objectives in this kind of work, which depends so much on the relationships and opportunities that develop in the course of the work. In a sense, it is the parties to the conflict who set the parameters, sometimes even the agenda, for the work, and the organisation must allow the mediator to have the flexibility to respond as the way opens.

A general objective of this work is to promote dialogue between parties in conflict who are not talking to each other; another is to reduce the suffering and bring the violence and injustice to an end. The methods of achieving these objectives may vary enormously in different situations. The best that the organisation can hope to do in the way of objectives may be to set some guidelines for the mediators that will help them to be able to respond quickly as opportunities for mediation arise, and to ensure that they are well-grounded in Quaker principles and what experience has taught in similar situations. Ultimately, the organisation must trust in the people they appoint to read the situation, to listen to the guidance of the Spirit, and to consult with others in the organisation as much as possible about the direction of the work.

Organisational professionalism

There is a need for Quaker organisations to support mediation work in a professional way. This means taking very seriously a decision to send mediators into a particular conflict. If the Religious Society of Friends decides to get involved in building relationships with political leaders in an attempt to facilitate a process of mediation, then there must be an organisational commitment to maintain this role as long as it might be useful. It is not fair to the parties involved for relationships of trust to be abandoned because of budgetary cuts or the departure of a particular mediator from the organisation. The supporting agency must make a long-term commitment, by planning to use its resources accordingly. A parallel commitment on the part of members of the Society of Friends might be a regular posing of the query: Am I willing to offer myself for service in work undertaken by Friends, or other agencies? Do I seek ways to prepare myself for such service?

Selecting the mediators

But how does the Quaker organisation select the people to do the mediation work? This question relates to previous chapters on qualifications, training and forming of teams. Many of those who have filled this kind of role over the years have been people in academic or professional positions which allowed them the freedom to travel for short-term missions. Others have been retired Quakers who have volunteered or been asked by the organisation to participate. A number of Quaker International Affairs Representatives have been involved in mediation as one aspect of their International Affairs role. People have come from diverse backgrounds, with varying levels of formal training, and much or little experience in the region, and have been able to undertake mediation.

Perhaps a kind of discernment process would be more appropriate than standard recruitment procedures in selecting potential Quaker mediators. The aim of the process would be to identify a team of people who would offer the right combination of personalities and skills, and who would be able to work together under demanding and stressful circumstances.

In some situations, the organisation has had a pool of people who could be drawn upon for mediation missions as the need arises. If Quakers are going to continue offering to do mediation, it may be necessary to look at how when other younger Friends can be identified and trained to become part of this pool of potential mediators. People in their 30's and 40's could be apprenticed with those in their 50's, 60's and 70's so that the skills and experience of the older generation of Quaker mediators are passed on to a new generation of Friends.

Links between Quaker representatives

There is a need for organisational links between the various Quaker representatives who are working in a mediating role in different situations and at different levels. Individuals who are actively engaged in this kind of sensitive role need to have the opportunity to discuss their work in a confidential way with other Quaker practitioners. Consultation and sharing of experiences can lead to opportunities for collaboration on a particular initiative, such as joint initiatives undertaken by Quaker United Nations Office (QUNO) staff and the Middle East Representatives. For the Quaker mediator, who may feel quite isolated and sometimes confused by the situation she is immersed in, the opportunity to share experiences, problems, doubts and fears with other Quaker mediators can give her new insights and perspectives as well as a level of personal support that is necessary to sustain the initiative.

QPS has had one consultation on political mediation, which brought together about 20 people with experience of mediation, both current and past, to share and analyse the experience and practices they had been engaged in. AFSC has had one gathering of their Quaker International Affairs Representatives (QIARs) in 1992. An annual meeting of QIARs was begun in 1953, but later replaced by meetings of the Quaker United Nations Group, involving staff and committee members related to the Quaker United Nations Offices in New York and Geneva, along with representatives of the Friends World Committee for Consultation (FWCC). Such meetings give the representatives an opportunity to get to know each other and to discuss issues and share concerns about their work. These are the kinds of connections that need to be institutionalised on a more regular basis, if the work done in the name of the Religious Society of Friends is really to be corporate work and not the work of isolated individuals and teams of mediators.

Links and communication between representatives and staff at various levels and in various locations are best coordinated from some central office which is able to keep in touch with all these workers. Sometimes an opportunity or a contact may happen at one of the Quaker UN offices, for example, that could be a helpful opening for Quaker representatives based in one of the field locations. Someone in the head office needs to recognise this fact and communicate it, as a matter of urgency, to the people in the field. QPS has recently formed a International Relations Unit in London which could be useful in this regard. The Secretary of the International Division at AFSC serves a similar linking function between the various areas of work in the world. FWCC, as an umbrella organisation for the world-wide family of Quakers and Quaker organisations, can also be a useful link for communication and networking.

How different kinds of work relate

The question of links between mediation work and other Quaker work is a very important organisational responsibility. Relief and development work in the region of mediation activity can form a strong base, as a manifestation of Quaker concern for victims of violent conflict. In Sri Lanka, Quaker Peace & Service trained village health workers, supported counselling for victims of violence, and provided escorts for relief supplies across the battle lines, as well as engaging in mediation. One way to see this is that the work on the ground lent credibility to the more diplomatic work.

It helped, I think, in terms of the community relations with people on the ground. Also, that QPS had workers in the east who were going back and forth across the lines helped to show that QPS was willing to take a risk, and not just fly in and out all the time in what might be seen as glory work.[122]

There can, however, be more tension between different kinds of work, even within the individual, and each is likely to see his or her own work as most important.

[The different kinds of work in Sri Lanka] complemented each other in a very concrete and perhaps necessary way, in that the other work you could always do, and it was a clear expression of compassion, and it also put you there in the war zone. It conflicted with the mediation work in that, when mediation gets a pace and the stakes are so high, it absorbs attention and gets a greater priority.[123]

If mediation always seems to be the organisation's highest priority, then other Quaker work in the area will no longer be seen as demonstrating a commitment to assisting the ordinary people in their suffering. If relief or development work is taken as highest priority, its needs may preclude some of the difficult contacts and confidential meetings that mediation often requires. Or, if Quaker relief or assistance in the area is perceived to be offered only to victims on one side, it can discredit the notion that Quakers are concerned about all sides in conflict. The committee that is making decisions about what work to undertake in a particular region must take these factors into account and, if possible, try to reach some kind of balance of work on the various sides. "Relief, development, and human rights work are important in and of themselves, and workers engaged in this work must not feel that theirs is less important than the more political or diplomatic work."[124]

Those involved in each kind of work need to be aware of other kinds of operations going on, but it would not be advisable to involve them directly in each other's work. For example, if it became known that development workers were organising meetings with political leaders or members of armed groups, the people they work with in a particular community might be compromised and endangered by this association. In some situations, at some moments, it may be necessary to focus exclusively on one kind of work — relief, development, human rights, or mediation — because the situation demands it.

A Quaker working in one region, which shall be nameless, became involved in facilitating dialogue among several groups that had previously been in conflict and did not trust one another. In order to make this facilitating role possible, the Quaker representative asked the sponsoring organisation to stop other work that would be seen as supporting one of the sides, particularly funding of groups on that side. In this case, a choice had to be made between two good approaches to work in the region.

For organisations as for individuals, reconciliation and advocacy, relief and development, may be in tension with each other, but this is a creative tension that requires equilibrium rather than the sacrifice of one component to another. Mediators expressed the strong view that organisations must, in the interest of integrity and the full living-out of their values, maintain overall balance by supporting all these kinds of work, but not necessarily in the same time and place.

Relating to the work of other (non-Quaker) organisations

Sometimes there may be a number of different organisations working in different ways on the same conflict situation. There is a need for the Quaker organisation to be aware of these other efforts and how they relate to the work that Friends are doing. It is possible that diverse initiatives might somehow complement each other, as is described in the following example from Rhodesia's transition to Zimbabwe.

In this case, there were three religious organisations working at different levels and in different ways. A Quaker team was shuttling around between the various political leaders, with guidance and support from Friends Service Council in London. Simultaneously, the Catholic Church and another group called Moral Re-Armament (MRA) were involved with other work both inside and outside Rhodesia, the Catholics emphasising moral pressure to change structures, MRA concentrating on individual conversions. Ron Kraybill, a Mennonite, describes the Quaker involvement in relation to what the other groups were doing.

The Quakers centered their activities around problems of process. The parties were not communicating clearly, and negotiation efforts were bedeviled by misinformation, misinterpretations, and lack of forums and mechanisms to communicate constructively. The Quakers sought to fill this gap, interpreting each side's concerns to others, conveying messages, trying to arrange face-to-face meetings, exploring options for resolution with parties informally at Lancaster House [talks in London] and elsewhere. Far more so than either the Catholics or MRA, the Quakers were involved in discussion of substantive issues with a broad range of leaders, and thus came the closest to a mediating role.

If the Quakers devoted the bulk of their attention to process problems, they were also directly concerned with both people and structure problems. Like MRA, they spent a great deal of time with individual leaders in a listening and supportive role. Like the Catholics, they demonstrated profound awareness of structural imbalances. Though they were careful not to endanger their mediation role through open activism, they interacted quietly with London-based groups which sought to highlight injustices in Rhodesia, and they sought to influence the British government to take what they felt were more enlightened approaches to the situation.

The groups [Catholics, MRA, and Quakers] focused upon different aspects of the problem – to some extent defined the problem itself differently – and thus employed differing strategies. But the effect of the three involvements was a complementary one. The Catholics and the Quakers recognised this and cooperated throughout the war years. But contacts between the MRA and the other two groups were minimal. This seems a regrettable gap: closer cooperation, particularly between the Quakers and MRA, might have substantially enhanced the work of both organisations.[125]

One wonders how many other situations where Quakers have gotten involved might offer a similar assessment - that "closer cooperation" with another organisation might have "substantially enhanced" the contribution that Friends were able to make toward resolving the particular conflict. It points up the need for someone in each organisation to be in touch with other groups and to keep the mediation team informed of any opportunities for cooperation with other groups.

<u>Beyond the work itself: recording and assessing</u>

And what happens to the records of all the confidential mediation meetings? Over all the years, and all the kinds of initiatives, there is clearly no single answer, but the following description by Joe Elder gives an example of two different treatments.

> The first time I met Adam [Curle] was in 1966, when AFSC and Friends Service Council [precursor of Quaker Peace & Service] decided they would jointly put together a team that would go to India and Pakistan. It was to be a British and American team sponsored by both groups. So it was Leslie Cross, who was FSC, and Adam who was in Harvard at the time, and I was AFSC. And that's all been written up. Mike [Yarrow] had time off to write the book about ten years later. And he asked if I had anything in my files that might be relevant. Well, I had all the notes I had typed from every interview. So, all I did was copy these and send them. He said it was like walking into the inner archives. [...]
>
> We had a final report, I think there was a short report and a long report, and we submitted them to both groups. But, for all the raw material, I don't think there was any particular procedure set up to keep it. It was just that I had stored all this stuff away.
>
> And now, on Sri Lanka, there must be a huge archive someplace, because we do submit all our notes.[126]

Documentation of this corporate experience is something that the organisations need to take seriously. Particularly in situations where there have been a succession of Quaker representatives or team members, clear documentation of what has happened in the past must be made available to new people coming into the work. Political figures who have been involved with the Quaker mediators will expect new people to have been fully briefed by their predecessors. The organisation must see that this does happen, not only through good documentation, but also by allowing for an overlap period between representatives. Otherwise, the continuity and momentum of the work can be lost.

There is also a need to maintain general records and documentation of mediation work done. There are at least two reasons for this. One is that acceptance of Quaker mediators depends in part on an assumption that each has somehow learned from the collective experience in other times and places, so it is important that this should be so. More attention needs to be devoted to writing case studies of situations, and drawing together mediators and potential mediators to learn by analysing cases, as was done in 1989 at the Old Jordans consultation.[127] A second reason is that committees, central staff, and others responsible for guidance and supervision of mediation projects need access to information about and lessons from other such situations.

Perhaps one of the more difficult tasks for the Quaker organisation is the assessment and evaluation of mediation work. This is particularly so, given that the results depend so much on the process itself and its development in a changing situation. In work that depends so much on relationships, there are not often tangible results that can be assessed or measured. The mere fact of having been asked to intervene may itself demonstrate a positive assessment of previous work and contacts. There are occasional, unsolicited testimonials from people involved in particular situations. The fact that busy political leaders continue to meet with Quakers and even request meetings can be an indication that the meetings are of some benefit to them. One can even count the number of times that meetings took place on each side, as has been done about the work of Quaker representatives in Berlin and Belfast, for example. But the quality of these meetings and the effect that they may have had on any improvement of the political situation are very hard to assess.

Sometimes a particular series of meetings may lead to some kind of agreement, written or unwritten, which improves the situation. Internally, the Quaker organisation may be able to point to this as an indication of some kind of effectiveness, but Friends must be very careful not to be claiming credit publicly for this agreement. The credit must be reserved for the parties who have made the agreement. If any of them choose to make a positive comment about the role of Quakers, this can be noted when evaluating the work. But, if these positive remarks are coming only from one side in the conflict, then questions need to be asked about whether the mediators are favouring that side in their approach to the situation.

At a more practical level, Quaker organisations, like others, have fund-raisers who are often looking for tangible activities they can cite to the funder of the work. One Quaker representative referred to these as the "nuggets" that illustrate the effectiveness of the work.

> The kind of nuggets are someone coming to me and saying: "I was sent to you because you really understand the situation in Sri Lanka." That's not meaning because of my intelligence in understanding it, but because they've been told there is somebody, and it's usually related to empathy, who understands it in that way.[128]

There is the danger that these "nuggets" could give misleading impressions about the quality or quantity of successes claimed by the organisation. At the same time, the pressure to provide startling anecdotes may endanger the confidentiality of the meetings, or the self-effacing role the mediators are at pains to carve out. Still, these incidents are some of the few available indicators that other people have judged that something valuable has come out of Quaker mediation efforts. Somehow, committees or others with oversight responsibility for mediation initiatives must attempt to evaluate them, not according to short-term gains or pressure to produce instant results, but having in mind some clear set of goals and standards. Work done under a sense of divine guidance should be done well, and implies a continuing testing as to whether there is guidance for the project to continue.

How and when to stop the mediation
A final responsibility for the organisation that is supporting a mediation initiative is to decide when it is time to withdraw from the effort and lay it down. A number of questions might be asked at this stage:

— Do all of the sides still accept the need for a third party
to be involved in this way?
— Has the situation itself changed dramatically, as by the
signing of an accord?
— What is the judgment of the representatives or the team who
are currently doing the work?
— Are the parties they have been working with able to meet
together now without the need for any third party
facilitation?
— Do the representatives and their supporting committee feel
that there is a mediating role that is still necessary
and that can be filled by Friends?
— Are there other organisations that have become involved and
that can fill the role more effectively?
— Have Quakers taken on a different role in the situation,
such as advocacy on behalf of one side, which makes it
more difficult to maintain the balance necessary for a
mediating role?
— Does this new role seem to be more important to the
situation at this time?
— Or has the situation changed in such a way that a new kind
of work, perhaps long-term community-based
reconciliation, is more appropriate now?

In deciding to lay down a piece of work, the supporting body will consider its own financial resources as well as its ability to find suitable personnel to continue the work. If the sponsoring body feels there is still a valid basis for this work, sufficient time must be allowed for appropriate people to feel called to offer service, and for the necessary funds to be found. But initiatives do finish, or become impossible, and work must be laid aside in order for new work to be taken up.

CHAPTER 12

Sometimes Failure or Futility

IT MAY BE BEGINNING TO SOUND as though any movement even to investigate the possibility of acting as mediator in a political conflict, leads to years of involvement and eventual settlement. But this is by no means the case.

Nothing happens
    Sometimes, possible opportunities to assist with mediation are declined at a very early stage. Sometimes, approaches may be so tentative that the person approached to act as mediator does not even realise that this is what was being asked, and declines by not seeing the opening. The individual or organisation approached may realise that something crucial is lacking on their part as the potential mediator: knowledge, standing, impartiality, or just time or personnel. Or, a serious assessment may be made, and the decision taken that mediation is not the appropriate way to intervene, or that the situation is for some reason unsuitable. Very often, timing is a significant factor, as in the QPS Uganda case, which will be described later in this section.
    The 1989 QPS consultation on political mediation included considerable discussion of how to discern when to undertake a mediation initiative, and produced the following statement:

> Mediation works best when all parties to the conflict have internal strengths and confidence, but may have reached a stalemate. The importance of establishing and maintaining contacts over a period, even of many years, was stressed, so that when the situation seems to open up for mediation, we may be known as credible and available. Ultimately, the question of timing may be a religious one – a kairos – or a moment of truth, divinely or intuitively revealed, but not amenable to explanation or analysis.[129]

This is a striking image, of people preparing years in advance for an opportunity that may never come, keeping up with events, writing to and calling on a range of people, holding themselves ready to be more involved if needed, but not imposing themselves at the time of their own choosing. Surely this is a religious enterprise, with so much greater likelihood of failure or futility than success. And it takes some odd combination of arrogance and humility, to think that one could be useful in someone else's conflicts, but to go about intervening in such an indirect and unassertive way.

Begun, but not completed

Once a mediation initiative begins, there are many more ways for it to end less than successfully, if by "success" we mean a peaceful settlement acceptable to the parties involved. Very often, while someone is shuttling between the sides, or even while negotiations go on, external circumstances change, and one side (or both) pulls out. This may be because of a change in the balance of power between them: one side feels either too weak to negotiate an acceptable outcome, or strong enough to win a complete victory. Or an atrocity occurs which makes settlement or even negotiation unacceptable to the party which has suffered; indeed, atrocities may often be committed for just this reason, to derail possible peace initiatives.

In Northern Ireland, for example, one could have predicted that an upsurge in violence was likely when interparty talks began in 1990-91, because a settlement was not in the interests of some of the paramilitary groups, who were not included in the talks. In fact, the number of deaths increased by half over the previous years. That situation had a particularly paradoxical dynamic, in that one group, the Loyalist paramilitaries, had declared a unilateral cease-fire when the first stage of talks began, but said explicitly that they would resume their violent campaign if the politicians were unable to reach a solution. So, during the following year, one side was engaging in violence because the talks kept breaking down, and the other because the talks looked sometimes as though they might succeed.

There are also internal reasons that mediation processes fail. A change in leadership of a grouping or government may bring in militarists, a more hard-line faction, or someone whose history makes it unthinkable for opponents to negotiate with him/them. (Or, of course, conversely, new leaders may make negotiations look more likely to succeed, as with the change in the Israeli government in 1992.)

Or, a leadership change may simply leave the mediators with no footing. Shuttle mediation by jet is particularly vulnerable to this sort of change, if the mediators depend on relatively few, high-level contacts. This is one reason, of course, that mediators usually try to maintain a range of contacts on all sides: both to develop a more complex sense of the views of each side, and so as not to depend too heavily on any individual contact. Adam Curle describes one situation in which Quakers were active as mediators, where an internal change dislocated the mediation for a time:

> There has been a change in sponsorship in our mission, so to speak. It started off with sponsorship by a man who was head of security. And he became a good friend. And he had been expecting to be either president or at least prime minister, when there was a change of government. Instead of that, he became Minister of Fisheries and Dried Meat, or something like that.[130]

In this case, it was possible to build new relationships with other people, but it took time, and sometimes this loss of contacts leaves the mediators unable to proceed at all. The same can be said, of course, if something should prevent the mediator from continuing. The process may be suspended until another mediator is found, or may even be halted altogether. This is one of the reasons that organisations sometimes build mediation teams, so that the process does not depend entirely on one person.

It is, of course, quite possible for mediation to fail because the goals, needs, or intentions of the parties are so incompatible as to make agreement impossible. In such cases, mediators may persevere for long periods of time, looking for openings, and hoping that other reconciliation attempts, proceeding in parallel, may produce changes that permit successful negotiations. Mediation occurs in the real world of violent conflict, among people who may be feeling frightened, angry, or wary, and in situations where leaders have very limited flexibility and control. So, the leader may be unwilling to negotiate settlements which would not satisfy his constituency, but simply lead to his overthrow and a continued conflict. Treachery is also possible, either by a direct party to the negotiations, or because an army or armed wing is almost never under the complete control of the leader. For all of these reasons, in all of these ways, mediation initiatives can fail at any stage. Mediators try to anticipate problems, and invent ways to circumvent them or deal with them, but failure is always likely.

Unintended results

As noted above, one issue in assessing the value of mediation is what is meant by success. Sometimes, what appears to have been an aborted attempt, may have unforeseen but important results. Adam Curle describes one situation, the civil war in Nigeria-Biafra, where mediation appeared to have failed entirely, and one army was victorious. In retrospect, it appears that the mediation initiative may have helped to make possible a healing peace, by changing the perceptions of the Nigerian Army's leaders. This army, in turn, behaved in a most unexpected fashion.

> Twice we thought we had a truce arranged; twice events on the battlefield aborted it. The war eventually ended militarily amid despairing fears of a massacre. But all predictions were wrong. Even now, I cannot speak without emotion of the way in which, instead of slaughtering the defeated Biafrans, the Federal Nigerian soldiers gave them food and money, cared for them, took them to hospitals, treated them as brothers in the most wonderful spirit of reconciliation. Quakers were told by several people, whose judgement was reliable, that Quaker work over nearly three years of educating the two sides about each other and de-demonizing both had filtered down from the leaders to the troops and contributed significantly to this miraculous outcome.[131]

It is, of course, comforting to think that one's efforts may not have been in vain, even if they do not appear to produce the intended result. But it is also the case that mediations fail, or do not take place at all, or that mediators, like the United Nations Middle East envoy in 1948, Count Folke Bernadotte, are killed in the attempt. At best, small and powerless groups like Friends can have some small role to play at some stage of a process. This can make it difficult for a Quaker organisation to decide whether to invest its limited resources and personnel in a mediation initiative, with very little likelihood of marked success, and the real chance of complete failure or futility. The example which follows shows a particular process, one organisation trying in good faith to decide whether to act in one situation, and may illustrate some of the many difficulties involved.

A case study: Uganda

At a given moment, individual Friends were approached and asked whether they could help resolve the conflict between a rebel army and the government in a particular area of Uganda. These individuals met with the requesting parties, to see what they had in mind, and then received permission to bring the issue to Quaker Peace & Service, as they felt that an organisational commitment would be necessary.

A small, ad hoc committee was established, and the decision eventually was made to send two people to investigate whether a mediation initiative was feasible. These two spent a few weeks in the area (it was by now a year after the original request), and reported to the East-West Africa Committee of QPS in London that they thought something might be possible. In the discussion of this report it was noted:

In favour of QPS involvement are the facts that we have been invited by those involved in the area, and that the task of conflict resolution is an appropriate concern. Some doubts were expressed about the feasibility of making contact with all the groups involved in such a complex conflict situation.[132]

So the Quaker committee had some doubts at this stage – a likely factor in delaying for many months the decision to proceed. A Uganda Mediation Support Group was formed in the interim. It was nearly two years after the initial request when they finally appointed two Quakers with experience of mediation and of Uganda to spend three months in Uganda, trying to begin a mediation initiative.

These Friends arrived in the area of conflict to discover that local people had decided to undertake the mediation initiative on their own. Since it took so long for the committee to decide and for people to be sent out, the local people had assumed that Friends were no longer interested in the initiative, and therefore did not contact QPS in London to ask for assistance. There had, in fact, been a point in the process when an outside organisation might have been helpful in offering a venue and funding for talks outside the country. This was one factor that brought the process to a halt.

During their three month period in Uganda, the two Quakers were able to help the local people to evaluate the process that they had been engaged in, and to bring in stories of what had happened in other situations. The local people had created a process of shuttling back and forth between the sides that was very similar to the way Quakers have done mediation in other situations, and were encouraged at being able to see their attempts in a larger perspective.

Some of the local mediators felt that the presence of experienced people from outside might be an impetus to revive the mediation process. So these Quakers made some initial contacts with people on each side, but it seemed that neither side was prepared to consider negotiation at that time. Both sides felt that they might have a chance to win militarily. The time for negotiation had passed, at least for the moment, but it was a changing situation, and the sides might later be more open to negotiation. The visiting Friends therefore encouraged the local people who had acted as mediators to maintain contacts with all sides, if they could, and to alert QPS if the situation changed.

84

A third Quaker joined the other two for the last two weeks of their time in Uganda, to help them assess the situation. They recommended to the committee in London that Friends should schedule a follow-up visit after a few months. After meeting with the three returning Quakers, the Uganda Support Group recommended that:

QPS should remain ready to respond to a request for a third visit by a pair of mediators. QPS should keep up communication with [other organisations'] representatives in Uganda, and with various contacts [the QPS representatives] had made, to assure them of our interest and support, and to keep a channel open for possible requests.[133]

The support group took a "wait and see" attitude, rather than recommending that a return visit be scheduled at that time. The representatives of other NGOs had been helpful with logistical support when the Quaker team were in Uganda, and had agreed to report when they were able to visit the area. The local mediators, however, were unlikely to contact London, since communication was quite difficult and dangerous about such sensitive matters.

Eventually, by now 2½ years after the original request, two staff members from London with no previous involvement in this situation did make a visit to the area, and met the local mediators again. One of the local people told them that Quakers had come too late, and they reported this back to the committee in London, who then agreed to lay down the initiative completely.

Following the staff visit [to Uganda] in April, which suggested that relief rather than mediation is what is needed now in the area, we agree that the Uganda Mediation Support Group should be laid down.[134]

So, in this case, timing of the intervention by Friends was a crucial factor, in a situation that changed rapidly. The opportunity to be helpful in the situation seemed to have been lost because the original request was slow in coming, the decision-making process took so long, and there was not sufficient communication with people in Uganda to convince them that Quakers were serious about wanting to assist with mediation. Not having representatives permanently in the area meant that QPS could not evaluate the changing situation, and those who went were seen by local people as arriving too late.

Another case study: mediation that did not happen

In another part of the world, where the Asia representatives of the American Friends Service Committee have been active, there is an example of assistance requested but not actually needed. It seems that the people involved thought that they needed outside help to organise peace negotiations. But, in fact, the process was able to proceed without this assistance from Friends.

Donna Anderton: The notion had arisen of a peace initiative to bring the two sides of that discussion to the table. We were approached and asked if we could be helpful in one of a couple of ways. If we could help handle logistics to have it outside the country, because it's illegal to belong to that group, so the government can't meet with them [in their own country].

And, if asked, would we be willing to facilitate those discussions? And we expressed our interest in that, and said what we bring to that is not expertise in the situation. The guy we know said: "Look, we aren't asking you because you're experts, we're asking you because you're Quakers and outsiders and we know you personally and trust you."......Now, what's happening is that the people who were arguing hardest for that are becoming involved in some of the actual negotiations. Some absolutely wonderful things have happened in the past couple of weeks, things that may make some openings. So, there are false starts in that sort of direction, too.

Sue: Oh, but that's not a false start. That's a thing which was a possibility, which may have made something else possible. The fact of having that as a possible offer may have precipitated a conversation in which somebody said: "Well, if we can talk to them outside the country, why don't we talk to them inside the country?" So I don't think that's a false start at all.

Donna: No, it was a way in which we were conversationally useful for a while. It's not at the fledgling stage any more, where we might have been useful, and that's wonderful.[135]

There must be innumerable cases of this sort, in which people were prepared to provide a service that was not finally requested. Some would conclude that the mediator should be more direct, and "sell" her services, showing the opponents how they need what she can offer. And there would be cases where this might work, and turn out to be very useful to those involved, because these are violent conflicts which cause great suffering, and because participants are often desperate to find ways to settle. But this is not the way Quakers work. In some paradoxical way, their refusal to promote their services is a mark of their amateur status, but based on the professional discipline and discretion that is at the very heart of the process they espouse.

Case Study: Quaker "failure" as part of a larger "success"

Quaker involvement in the transition to black-majority rule in Zimbabwe (formerly Rhodesia) has been documented elsewhere.[136] Ron Kraybill offers this assessment of the Quaker efforts.

The Quaker involvements in Rhodesia are, at one level, a study in failure as a fundamental aspect of peacemaking. The Quakers invested heavily in four major efforts to set up meetings among top leaders, all of which failed to materialize. [...]

The Quakers focused on perceptions and processes that would enable a negotiated settlement. In the end the parties reached this goal at Lancaster House [in London], rendering the work of the Quakers almost invisible against the backdrop of larger success. Their work so closely matched the complex fabric of influence moving the parties toward Lancaster House that it is impossible to isolate the Quaker contribution from that of other actors. [...]

There are times when nothing clarifies like failure. President [Julius] Nyerere [of Tanzania] was angry and let-down by the Rhodesian air strikes against Lusaka [Zambia] that coincided with the messages that Quakers were conveying between him and [Bishop Abel] Muzorewa. But having failed in his effort to work cooperatively with Muzorewa through the good offices of the Quakers, he was prepared a few weeks later to issue a ringing call for the British to convene the Lancaster House negotiations. It is likely that this Quaker-assisted failure contributed to the evolution of Nyerere's decisive stance.

Precisely the difficulty "proving" success illustrates an important characteristic of many religious peacemakers. The Quakers intentionally operated in such a way that their own contribution to any success would be invisible. They made no effort to hide their role, but they sought to be genuine servants to the interests of others, and they understood that their ability to contribute depended on keeping Quaker interests minimal. After all, earning the trust of parties, which is often the hardest part of mediating in cases such as this, depends upon a commitment to the interests of the parties that is unadulterated by the need for "credit".[137]

This assessment resonates with the experience of other Quaker mediators. Their efforts are sometimes most successful precisely because they do not need to claim any success. Invisibility of the mediator becomes a virtue. Sometimes the mediator may become the scapegoat for a failed initiative, but this failure pushes one or more of the parties to try something else that proves to be more successful. In all cases, the Quaker role is just one small piece of the "complex fabric of influence" that leads the sides to come together. A willingness to try and fail in the short-term may lead to a larger success in the long-term.

CHAPTER 13

Confidentiality and Truth

THE NEED FOR A LEVEL OF confidentiality in this kind of work presents some dilemmas for the Religious Society of Friends, which has a testimony about truthfulness and honesty in all dealings. John Woolman, who is probably the best-known Quaker advocate of truth in all business and personal affairs, was very clear that, in "the urgency of affairs", one should not say to oneself: "I must needs go on, and in going on I hope to keep as near to the purity of Truth as the business before me will admit of."[138] He is saying that the first priority should be truth, not the urgency of the situation or the needs of the work. So the question must be asked of Quaker mediation: can confidentiality and truth be compatible?

Confidentiality in mediation work means that the content, and sometimes even the fact, of a meeting or conversation will not be revealed openly and publicly. This information is reserved for a limited number of people whom the parties involved agree to, either explicitly or implicitly. In the overall process, this is usually still the pre-negotiation phase, where the parties are not yet in direct, public contact with each other. Indeed, the usefulness of this kind of mediation is that it permits opponents to learn more about each other, and to modify their own positions as they begin to understand each other's reactions, before going public. People on their own side, even people in their own groupings, may not realise that informal, indirect contact exists. Leaders may feel that their own people won't yet understand the need for such contact with the enemy, or might not yet be supportive of it. The mediator offers the possibility of communicating through a third party, without publicity, before negotiations are ready to begin.

The move to negotiations may depend on changes in external circumstances, on one or both sides gaining confidence in their own position, or on the participants building sufficient trust in each other and the process — the latter being the principal work of the mediator. At this delicate stage, any publicity may wreck the possibility of further contact, and may, indeed, expose participants to verbal or even physical attack, if their own side sees them as traitors.

Confidentiality is a limiting of what can be revealed about meetings. In its most extreme form, it constrains parties not to say anything. But, generally, mediation is a process of communication. In the early stages, the communication is indirect, through the mediator, in conversations with each side about other viewpoints. In some cases, there may be a specific message to be carried to someone in an opposing faction or government. Often the discussion with the intermediary is totally off-the-record and not for attribution directly, but there is an implicit understanding that the mediator may share the ideas being considered with people on the other side, in order to get their reactions. For most of these people, the particular concern is that the details of the meeting not become public through the news media. Sometimes they are also concerned that people at other levels on their own side not know of a particular meeting or proposal while it is still at a very sensitive stage and might alarm some of the more cautious people in their own camp.

For the mediator, this means the obligation to consider carefully what each party wishes to convey to the other, as well as what each wishes to learn. Sometimes, someone states clearly what seems to be the intended message, and for whom. More often, what is intended is a more general sharing of views and possibilities, and the mediator's particular asset is to carry an understanding rather than a direct quote, without authority to act on behalf of either party. This means that, if the message causes offense, it can be explained or corrected without either party losing face.

Is strict confidentiality necessary?

There is not consensus among Quaker mediators about the need for strict confidentiality. Some mediators describe confidentiality as the bedrock of their work, the one real requirement, without which political figures will refuse to meet with them. Mike Yarrow sees confidentiality as an advantage of unofficial third parties, because they are able to "operate outside the public limelight and with the least possible need for public recognition."[139]

The mediator may be able to promise not to reveal information, but has less control over the actions of other parties. H W van der Merwe has been involved in facilitation of communication between political groups in South Africa, while he has also been director of the Centre for Intergroup Studies at the University of Capetown. When he arranges a meeting between adversaries, he does not ordinarily promise secrecy. Instead, he encourages the participants to alert others on their side in advance, if they are worried about reactions.

> My staff all know about it. So, it's not a secret, but not made known publicly. Now, I'm comfortable about that, because [the participants] also cannot come and expect to have completely secret meetings in my office. Surely this kind of thing becomes known.... And the best you can do is to protect their integrity, so they don't get too embarrassed.... Either you must say it's completely secret and doesn't leak out, or you must say there is no way we can keep this secret, so we must now start working on how to handle it. If it's going to leak out through second or third sources, is it better that we make it known to those people whom we are concerned if they hear about it?[140]

An example from Sri Lanka suggests that mediators sometimes have to accept a limited amount of publicity about what they are doing. Here, the Quakers were careful not to publicise their visits, but reports were published in local papers, including some inaccurate information.

Because we are not publishing anything, when something is published [by some-one else], we make a point to write and say that we are very disappointed. In this case, I wrote to [people on all the sides involved], and said that "I do not know who gave this information, but I very much regret that this is being pub-lished like this. And some of it is incorrect." None of them have taken offense to that. They appreciate that we object to self-publicity. This is, in fact, a strength. They publish in Jaffna, but they don't publish any details of what we discuss. But [a contact in Jaffna] said, "Look, people want peace. People know that you have come as a peace mission. We have no total control on the news-papers. They write what they like. They will go to the hotel manager and take your names from there, and they will say that this particular peace delega-tion came. Then I am coming to your hotel to see you, and they all know who I am. So they will say that I came and I spoke to you. I cannot give you a guarantee that this will not be published." I had to accept this.[141]

Quaker conferences and diplomats' meetings often have rules of confidential-ity, usually specifying that participants may not quote others or attribute statements or views to them, nor even identify the event, who was there, who sponsored it. But many participants report back to their own organisations[142] and therefore complete secrecy is difficult to promise. What is possible is what Everett Mendelsohn calls "a degree of opaqueness from the public", that the participants' words would not be quoted. If com-plete secrecy were required, one would not use this kind of semi-public meeting, but a much more restricted setting.

Some Quaker mediators will be in contact with representatives of governments and other non-governmental organisations concerning the particular conflict situation.

Well, in almost every situation I've been in, there has been contact between the Quaker team and a lot of other organisations - people in government, people in various embassies, people in the UNICEF office, FAO office, churches, uni-versities and so on - a great network of people who to a greater or lesser extent exchange information and discuss things.[143]

It may be important to keep in touch with governments, with international organisa-tions such as the UN and the Commonwealth Secretariat, and any other organisations that have an interest or involvement in the situation. In some cases, they could be seen as parties to the conflict, if they are supporting one of the sides. Or, they could be help-ful in providing introductions if they have contact with people that the Quaker team are needing to meet. But it is necessary for the mediators to exercise discretion in their shar-ing of information, so as not to jeopardise the process at a delicate stage. Diplomats have been known to leak information to journalists or to mention at a cocktail party some-thing that had been shared in confidence.

Although Quaker mediators may enjoy for some time the luxury denied to high-profile negotiators, of holding meetings and carrying messages without publicity, they must understand that this is not guaranteed, and that someone may make information public at any stage. Indeed, if confidentiality is seen as being so crucial to the success of the work, it can offer a weapon to the unscrupulous.

Our bluff was called, that we would stop if there was publicity about it. There was publicity, and it was clearly by somebody trying to disrupt the process. Everybody else seemed to say: "Forget it, just keep at it." But it's a problem.[144]

It is important, then, to be realistic in promises of confidentiality, and to realise that the trust and the relationship between people have probably, over time, become more important than promises of confidentiality or impartiality. This work of political mediation involves violent, deadly disputes between implacable enemies. It will probably have to withstand atrocities, deception, and the violation of cease-fires. While confidentiality is an original intention and a worthwhile parameter, the process will need to be resilient enough not to collapse irretrievably at the first breach.

Confidentiality in relation to other Quaker work

The tensions described earlier between different kinds of work can be exacerbated by mediation's need for such strict confidentiality. While one may see these as generally creative, positive tensions, they may be harmful if they cause individuals or organisations to sacrifice one important area of work to another. Probably the best one can do is to recognise the likelihood of such tensions, try to live with them creatively, and commit oneself to use as spiritually-rooted a process as is possible in deciding between options that are mutually exclusive.

I could see us saying: Well, the off-the-record, totally confidential nature of these [contacts] is really getting in the way of the form of peace education we really want to engage in, which is also deeply pacifist. I might say: "All right, we might have to give up those involvements in confidential things, if we judge this other to be important". I can imagine that. But I would insist on having it be informed by that same commitment to nonviolence and what it means about how you work with two parties. This is the kind of thing that's been the classic strain on some of the work here.[145]

Confidentiality in reporting

A significant issue for the mediator is the level of reporting within her own organisation. In most cases, Quaker mediators do not take notes during a sensitive meeting, but will later make notes of the conversation as a record of what was discussed. These confidential notes might be used as a reminder of what issues needed to be conveyed to someone else and what issues needed to be pursued further at a future meeting with the same party. The notes might be shared with one or two others in the organisation - committee members or staff members, as appropriate - but would go no further than that. In other cases, mediators have sometimes made a written note after a meeting and then shown it to the party or parties involved to check it for accuracy. This note would be seen by all members of the mediation team and perhaps one or two others in the organisation, and might provide a basis for discussion with a party on an opposing side in the conflict.

At the next level of reporting, most members of the committee overseeing the work might see a less confidential report from the mediation team, with a more general summary of whom the team has met and what have been the broad areas of discussion. In some cases, specific names may be left out of this report. Beyond that level, the wider Society of Friends and the Quaker funding agencies might see a report with no names mentioned and only a very general description of the on-going work of the representatives, with perhaps more emphasis on the public side of the role rather than the confidential contacts. In some cases, it is judged unwise at the time even to acknowledge that an initiative is going on in a particular area, because doing so might endanger local contacts. It is understandable that one would give priority to the safeguarding of life, but it is important that the Society of Friends as a whole should know, in a general way, that this is so, and that certain pieces of work will therefore not be reported as widely or as freely as usual, until the situation permits.

In all of this reporting, the mediators do not, or should not, falsify or distort the information in such a way as to make it an un-truth. But they do generalise the information so as not to reveal any confidential facts about meetings or discussions which, if they were made public, could endanger or discredit the parties involved. Sometimes the information is only confidential for a period of months or a few years until the parties feel ready to meet and discuss these issues more openly. In other cases, there is information that is never revealed publicly while the parties involved are still alive, or at least while they're still active on the political scene, but it does become part of an archival record of the work.

And truth?

John Woolman's statement describes a range of dilemmas confronting the mediator, of which confidentiality is only one. In the nature of the role, with its requirements of transparency within relationships and opaqueness with respect to publicity, the mediator must expect to have conflicting pressures.

There is a kind of minimalist position, that one must at the least refrain from telling untruths. There would be consensus on this requirement, though it might have behind it a reservation to fit extraordinary circumstances. If one were protecting a fugitive from what seemed to be an unjust law, would truth require that one should say so directly if asked by the security police? If a mediator was visited by military authorities and asked directly for the whereabouts of an insurgent leader she had met with earlier that day, would truth require her to disclose the location, believing that the military would use this information to go there to kill the person? And if the paramilitary leader asked the whereabouts of the army commander, in order to have him killed? These are not entirely far-fetched questions, as contemporary mediators do find themselves in situations where they have information that might endanger the life of another. Most seem to come down on the side of protecting life, though they try to do so without lying. If the interrogator is a known person, perhaps a leader with whom a relationship exists, the response often is to re-state the role of the mediator, and the need to move freely between the sides. As with so many dilemmas, these seem not to be susceptible to solution by rules; instead, mediators apply the principles and approaches they generally use, and this usually seems to work.

A more refined position on truth, befitting the role adopted by a mediator, is that she must avoid the temptation to agree with what people say on one side for the sake of harmony and then to agree with a quite different statement or interpretation of events on the other side. Sydney Bailey sees this as crucial to working between Israel and Arabs in the Middle East, for example, when he says: "I think the important thing is that we don't say different things to different parties."[146] Roland Warren, when he was Quaker International Affairs Representative in Berlin, stressed the need for this kind of consistency with both sides:

> One of the QIAR's working in both parts of the divided Germany made it a deliberate point never to say, or agree to, anything on one side of the Berlin Wall which he was not willing to say, or agree to, on the other side. This turned out to be a difficult, but important discipline.[147]

It is an important discipline, and part of the transparent honesty that many Quaker mediators aspire to, to listen to their own statements as though all sides could hear them, and be sure that they would be willing for each side to know what they have said to the other. Because of the polarisation, the distrust, the vastly different experiences and perceptions, speaking the same truth to all sides is a great challenge, but an integral part of the role.

At many levels, in many ways, mediators are confronted with dilemmas that have to do with truth and confidentiality. What to reply when a border official asks the purpose of your visit? How to answer journalists who notice your movements? What to do when one contact asks you point-blank whether you set up a recent meeting? In these, and many other situations, mediators must grapple with the requirements of different, but important values. Committees and organisations can be helpful, in assisting the mediator to think in advance about dilemmas that may arise, and in both challenging and supporting decisions made. Ultimately, at the moment of decision, mediators will have to rely on their consciences and their experience. Everett Mendelsohn describes the issue this way:

> I do ask myself, very consciously, what is the non-violent or the pacifist imperative here? When you're in a situation where there's a question: Should I tell someone something, or hold it back? Should I be fully honest, or only partially informative? And those are often the things that come up in the interaction.
>
> "Who was telling you that?" you hear them asking. They may not ask it directly, because they don't want to be told: "No, I can't tell you." But, should I keep diverting?
>
> And, in that way, I continually check back and say: "What is the nature of the honesty in this position which is living out that fuller role that you've attempted to adopt, of being engaged in peace-making and non-violence?"[148]

Fundamentally, it is not so important to satisfy the minimalist position, the letter of the law, by refraining from outright lies. What is important is to live the truth, and to try to enable others to find the courage to do the same, each of us holding to the truth as we know it, and listening carefully for the truth we do not have, the truth held by those most different from us.

Hard truths

In trying to clear up misunderstandings, to erode stereotypes, and to refine the ability to assess others' actions and reactions, mediators will often act as interpreters. Because they know political leaders who do not know each other, mediators may be able to help them to put each other's statements and gestures in context, to explain how the speaker uses words or to describe the history behind his actions, and in various ways to improve their communication. One must, however, resist any urge to soften or hedge the truth. It might be possible to justify it to oneself with the notion that a softer version will be easier for the opponent to accept, but this is sacrificing a long-term goal for a short-term convenience. These people are refusing to meet with each other, perhaps trying to kill each other; if that is to be changed, it will require dealing with hard feelings, harsh statements, and a history of pain and suffering.

> This conflict is not going to be resolved through good intentions. It's going to be resolved by some very hard negotiations, the beating of heads together.[149]

> The parties need to recognize that they are enemies, and not try to act like friends. And you have to start there, for negotiations to succeed. You don't negotiate with your friends, you give things to your friends. You negotiate with your enemies.[150]

This is another situation where the mediator can model the behaviour expected of the parties to the conflict, by a willingness to hear the true depth of the other's feelings, and to try to make that the basis of a relationship. Facing the truth, the hard edge of hatred and pain, will not destroy the process, but will make it worthwhile.

CHAPTER 14

Motives for Mediation Work

IN LOOKING AT THE EXPERIENCE OF Quakers who have been engaged in mediation work, one should not neglect to analyse the motives for doing this work. Individuals who fill this role may each have their own reasons for wanting to be involved, and one hopes that some of them are based on Quaker principles. The supporting organisation will also have its motives for involvement, some of which may be made explicit in stated goals and objectives for the work, and some of which may be less obvious, even to the people doing the work.

Why do you do mediation?

Perhaps it might be good to begin with some personal responses to this question from individual Quakers who have been involved in mediation work. H W van der Merwe describes a personal characteristic as his motivation.

> I don't think it's because people asked me to do it, it's just a natural inclination. In Zimbabwe, in Southern Rhodesia, where I was a missionary, my African name was Multi Worugare, the Maker of Peace. I just naturally... If I read in the paper about a conflict, I have an urge to go and see the people. If it's strangers I don't know, I just wish I could settle the matter.[151]

John McConnell speaks in somewhat similar terms about feeling that he wants to do something about conflict - something that is consistent with his values and beliefs. He suggests that his is a visceral response to the suffering and death caused by wars.

> When I read about suffering caused by conflict in the papers, [...] I feel nauseated, and want to do something about it. If I wasn't a committed pacifist, I could say: 'Send in the army' and be satisfied. But one needs to find an approach that is compatible with one's beliefs and values.
>
> I find I tend to repress awareness of the suffering of others: given the magnitude of needless suffering and the effectiveness of the media in conveying it, one can't live even moderately happily without doing so. At the same time, however, I want to do something about it and this is the something that I can do!

Actually, when I have been involved in mediation initiatives, I have felt a real process to be there that is not strange to me and in which I can actually be of help. Peacemaking is inherently uncertain - maybe it will bear fruit and maybe it won't - but at the same time one is absolutely certain that it **ought** to be taking place.[152]

Joe Elder offers three different kinds of motivation. The first is that of a scholar, with an academic interest in the area of conflict.

Well, anybody's motivation, one could go back to psycho-analyzing oneself... As an academic, it's the greatest excuse to step into the middle of the way this thing operates.

The second is the possibility of being involved in preventing or ending rather than repairing the ravages of war.

In terms of where I think Quakers ought to be, this seems to be exactly where Quakers ought to be. You look at the relief efforts and all of that, and I've seen some of that, enormous amounts of work to take care of people battered up in the Vietnam War and so forth. If there is any way an effort could be placed to prevent or terminate this, then that probably is the most important pressure point or point of contact.

The third is the organisation's return on investment.

To put personnel and committed action, it just seems in terms of pay-off you can't think of anything that could be more significant. Then you look at the success rate, which isn't all that impressive... But, for a small group, with limited resources, it just seems as though there's probably more return for effort in whatever the abstract sense is, in preventing the loss of life and maintaining dialogue, and getting people to develop some sort of trust and contact with each other.[153]

In these different but related ways, Quakers as individuals and as groups have been moved to offer to act as mediators.

What are the rewards of mediation?
C.R. Mitchell has provided a framework or paradigm which might be helpful for this analysis of motivations. He suggests that institutions undertake an intermediary role in a conflict because they obtain some reward for doing so, and then goes on to distinguish between benefits accruing from three distinct aspects of the intermediary's role. These are benefits derived from:

(1) engaging in the behaviour of an intermediary, irrespective of outcome (process rewards);

(2) achieving some form of settlement of the dispute in question which is at least minimally satisfactory to the parties (achievement rewards); and
(3) achieving a particular, sought-after settlement which, apart from at least minimally satisfying the parties, also advances the interests of the intermediary (settlement rewards).[154]

For most of the mediation work done under the auspices of Quaker organisations, the rewards would fall into the first category. Many of the conflicts where Quakers have taken a mediating role are situations that have not been resolved to the satisfaction of all the parties involved. The conflict between India and Pakistan over the territory of Kashmir has still not been resolved. The wall between East and West Germany came down in 1989, but there are still divisions to be healed. The Nigeria-Biafra war resulted in a military victory for the Nigerian side, hardly the desired result for the Biafrans. The conflict in Northern Ireland continues, although relationships have changed over the years. The Palestinian-Israeli conflict also continues. In all these cases, it would be hard for Friends to find rewards, other than process rewards, from their involvement in the situation. In the quotation cited above, John McConnell emphasises the importance of introducing a "real process", which may or may not bear fruit.

But what are the "process rewards" that Friends can find in doing mediation? There is the positive feeling that one gets from being able to provide a communication link between two people who had not previously been willing to speak with each other. The reward may be greater if the mediator succeeds in getting the parties to sit down together and begin to form a direct relationship with each other.

There is also the reward that one gets from being in contact with "important" people and being able to gain access to them at short notice. It can give one a feeling of importance oneself to have regular contact with influential people. This is seductive, and offers a major trap for mediators. Being greeted by famous people in the House of Commons tea room is gratifying, but is not the point of the mediator's work, and may impede that work. Important people are aware of being used, and are already sceptical of the mediator's ability to hold anything in confidence. Greater confidence is inspired by a more poised and matter-of-fact demeanour, with the mediator able to deal in a businesslike way with people with a vast range of backgrounds and influences.

At a moral and humanitarian level, mediators may derive satisfaction from being able to convince parties that it is better to try to resolve their differences through negotiations rather than through killing each other. Sometimes these humanitarian motivations stem from a concern for those who are deprived or oppressed because of the conflict situation.

While I deplore selective concern based on partisan politics, I sympathise with selective concern based on humanitarian feelings. Bias towards the deprived and oppressed characterises all humanitarian intervention. Unofficial mediators usually have strong humanitarian motivations and a natural sympathy with the deprived or wronged. Quakers, internationally, have traditionally sided with the underdog, and in South Africa interventions by British and South

African Quakers have consistently been inspired by the plight of the underdog. During the Anglo-Boer War, Quakers sympathised with the Boers and at present they assist blacks.

This kind of sympathy could easily lead to partisan intervention, in the sense that the deprived are seen as morally right or superior and the oppressed are equated with evil. Mediation between oppressor and oppressed therefore presents a special challenge to mediators with strong humanitarian concerns.[155]

There are a smaller number of cases in which it could be said that Quakers have accrued some achievement rewards. One is the involvement of Friends as intermediaries in the conflict in what was Southern Rhodesia which led to the formation of the independent state of Zimbabwe. Quakers have been credited with playing a part in the settlement that was concluded in the Lancaster House talks. Those Quakers who were involved have referred to a number of unsolicited testimonials from politicians and diplomats who were part of this talks process.

Mitchell's third category — settlement rewards — are often the benefits that are sought by governments which get involved as intermediaries in hopes of influencing the outcome of a conflict. But it is also possible that an individual Quaker or a Quaker organisation might have some interest in influencing the outcome of a particular conflict situation. Although Friends may not take sides, they may have a commitment to a particular process that they believe to be right for the situation. Most of the Quaker mediation work is undertaken with the assumption that dialogue between the sides is a good thing in itself and is what we hope to achieve. At certain stages of a conflict, one side or another may favour dialogue as a way of postponing change or entrenching the status quo, while at other stages the same group may be opposed to dialogue as lending credibility to an unworthy opponent. Both the motivation and the commitment of the mediator need to be more long-term, based on principle rather than current strategy.

Motivated by self-interest?

Zartman and Touval cite "self-interest" as a motive for mediation:

> In view of the considerable investment of political, moral, and material resources that mediation requires, and the risks to which mediators expose themselves, the motives for mediation must be found in self-interest as well as in humanitarian impulses....
>
> Even when they seek peace in the abstract, they [mediators] try to avoid terms not in accord with their own interests, although those interests usually allow for a wider range of acceptable outcomes than the immediate interests of the parties.[156]

To what extent is a Quaker mediator motivated by self-interest in doing this kind of work? Does she desire the excitement of being in a war situation, or the perceived influence that comes from contact with important people? Does she want to make a name for herself and be able to claim some credit for mediating a particular settlement? Is she planning to write a book or go on a lecture tour? Joe Elder, in the quotation above, has mentioned his academic interest in wanting to understand the conflict situation by stepping into "the middle of the way this thing operates". The authors of this book did not get involved in mediation in order to write about it, but that is nonetheless the result, with concomitant gains for ego or prestige.

And what about the organisations that support Quaker mediation work: do they have some interest in a particular outcome to the conflict? Do they want to gain more influence with one or more of the parties? What is the source of rewards for the Religious Society of Friends in undertaking this kind of work?

<u>What are the benefits?</u>

In addition to the three categories of rewards mentioned above, C.R. Mitchell also distinguishes between the following sources of rewards:

1. Benefits derived from having some effects on the conflict itself which includes those from the changed interaction between erstwhile adversaries, but also benefits derived from the parties themselves.
2. Benefits from affecting the regional environment within which the conflict is taking place.
3. Benefits from affecting other third parties involved in the overall structure of the conflict, such as allies and patrons of one of the adversaries, affected others or part of an international audience.
4. Benefits from affecting one's constituency, whether this is the salient interests in the political community of a governmental intermediary, or salient blocs and factions within the overall membership of an international or regional organisation.[157]

It is probably easiest to identify the benefits from having some effect on the conflict itself. In many situations, Quaker mediators or representatives have been able to bring some politicians together to meet directly; in some cases this has preceded direct negotiations, and in some cases the politicians have formed relationships that have continued without the need for a mediator. In South Africa, H W van der Merwe saw the results of meetings he had arranged between Afrikaners and the ANC leading to the decision by that group of Afrikaners to join formal negotiations involving the ANC. There are rewards to be derived from a reduction of violence between the "erstwhile adversaries" or a decision not to use violence. Adam Curle's description of the unexpectedly conciliatory end to the Nigerian civil war has already been cited. Even in unintended results, one does at least see results, and these can be something that keeps mediators committed to their work.

But what of the less direct benefits of mediation? Benefits derived from affecting the regional environment and from affecting other third parties are probably best seen in the situations where Quaker bodies have been instrumental in organising conferences related to conflict regions of the world. Quaker work in the Middle East in recent years has included a conference component which has brought together representatives of the parties in conflict along with representatives of their respective allies. Brewster and Anne Grace have described the conferences they have organised as a "vehicle" for meeting people on all sides and bringing them together. The rewards one gets from contacting politicians and governments may be multiplied when one is organising a large conference. Some of this Middle East conference work has involved the Quaker representatives at the United Nations and has thus had benefits for their relationships and credibility with delegations at the UN.

The benefits from mediation that are derived from affecting one's own constituency can be seen in some of the recent Quaker involvement in the Middle East during the Gulf War. While the governments of the United States and Great Britain were engaged in a UN-sanctioned war against Iraq, representatives of both AFSC and QPS maintained communication and contact with their countries' "enemy". Anne Grace visited Baghdad and reported on the situation and perspective from inside Iraq. This first-hand information from the other side was used in trying to inform and influence opinion among the "home" constituency of these Quaker bodies, as well as the wider public. An article she wrote at the time was circulated worldwide through international news services.[158]

Reinforcement

In addition to the motives that prompt people to become mediators, experience brings reinforcements that cause them to remain open to the possibility of acting as mediators.

Fundamentally, we act as mediators out of a sense of calling, with the aim of change in the political domain. Reinforcement to continue comes from within, as confirmation that the call continues, and from without, as confirmation that our actions produce the desired result.

Our actual experience is that reinforcement takes a variety of forms. At its most direct, it is expressed by those we work with: the members of political parties, armed groups, community groups. Sometimes, they simply say quite directly that the work and the process are valuable to them. More often, we infer their appreciation from their continuing availability and willingness to meet.

Affirmation also comes in the "frisson", the intuitive thrill one experiences when an important connection is made. This may be the moment when one political actor visibly breaks through to an understanding of another's situation, or when people meet and make a real connection that permits empathy and relationship-building. It may come when a politician suddenly seems to understand what mediation could offer, or when he accepts the risk of entering into dialogue with an opponent. There is also a negative kind of chill, when one sees that the process does not remain within the control of the mediator. Instead, the political actors have the freedom to draw their own inferences, and may use the knowledge in their own way.

There is also a spiritual motivation, which seems to come occasionally from events, but much more often from <u>relationships</u>. We often hold up pragmatism as a more useful political approach than rigid fundamentalism or narrow party defensiveness, and we feel that the process would work better if people behaved more pragmatically. But we recognise the rare capacity of individuals to transcend pragmatism, and we appreciate the moment when a politician acts on his faith. The relationships mediators have with some of the parties to the conflict are the best affirmation, in that many of these relationships have a clear spiritual/moral/ethical dimension. Particularly in a long-term relationship, there is an opportunity to appeal to something idealistic or spiritual in the politicians. Many ignore this aspect, or don't trust it; others somehow seem to want to be around it, even though they don't trust it enough to act on it; and some articulate it, even if in different terms.[159]

<u>Queries</u>
In concluding this discussion of motives for mediation, perhaps it would be appropriate to suggest a possible list of queries to be answered by any Quaker or Quaker organisation that is considering a possible mediation role. Both the organisation and the individual will have hidden as well as explicit motives, and some hard-headed questioning will be needed to unearth them and examine them carefully. Motivation is not the only issue in undertaking mediation, but it is one that is tested early and thoroughly, because parties to conflicts often have long experience of people coming with hidden agendas and of misguided attempts to sort out their conflict.

1. Why do you feel led or called to undertake a mediating role in this particular conflict situation?
2. What has been your previous involvement or interest in this situation? Do you foresee any conflict of interest?
3. What benefits or rewards do you hope to gain from this activity, including spiritual, psychological, professional or material rewards?

The responses from several Quakers which began this chapter suggest that people often have very personal reasons for wanting to be mediators. The process rewards may be adequate for the mediator, but it should be recognised that, for the parties in conflict, some result or achievement in settling the conflict is what benefits them. The mere fact of a process does not end the violence and suffering.

CHAPTER 15

Choosing Mediation

WHEN A DECISION IS TAKEN TO become involved in a specific situation in a mediating role, does this imply a particular view of conflict? Does the choice of mediation as the form of intervention have any influence on the possible results? By choosing mediation, are Friends imposing their own value system on the situation?

Many of those who have been engaged in mediation work would say that conflict is not necessarily a bad thing. It can lead to a kind of creative tension in a stagnant, unhealthy situation that forces people to question assumptions and consider change. But the kinds of conflict that are being considered here are conflicts that have gone beyond any kind of benign, creative tension and have exploded into violence, fear, and polarisation. Is there a danger that a positive view of conflict might lead to a more optimistic assessment of possibilities for mediation than the situation actually warrants?

Mediation is only one possible form of intervention in a political conflict. Other choices include: taking sides with one party whom we believe to be the "right" side, perhaps to the extent of joining that party or side; assisting a weaker party to become stronger in order to balance the power in this situation, possibly through coalition-building on that side; appealing to some authority or people of influence to impose a particular solution on the parties concerned; empowering local people to be able to make their own form of intervention by offering them training in conflict resolution skills; or just doing nothing.

Assumptions

The choice to do mediation implies a belief that the use of dialogue is better than the use of force or influence or pressure in resolving disputes. The assumption is that the parties will all be better off in the long-run if they can reach agreement through a kind of problem-solving approach in which basic needs are identified and a solution sought which meets all of them. The role of the mediator is somehow to encourage the parties to listen to each other's point of view and take these into account as they try to find an acceptable solution.

But do those engaged in the conflict really agree with these underlying assumptions? It is quite possible that they will agree to participate in the process, but may not accept the premises of the mediator. They may see mediation as a way of getting a respectable third party to legitimise their position of power and influence in the situation. Or they may intend to use the process to wrong-foot the opponent, manoeu-vering him into a position where there is no acceptable option open to him. This doesn't necessarily mean that mediation is wrong, but that the mediator must be careful that the differences in assumptions don't undermine the process which she is engaged in. She must be very firm and explicit with the parties that she is not interested in affirming a situation of unequal power. It also means that timing is a vitally important aspect of mediation: there are times when mediation seems the right approach, and other times when one side or another, or the mediator herself, may feel that mediation is not the best approach. H W van der Merwe, who usually describes what he does as "facilita-tion", recounts a process where the time for mediation arrived.

> There has been some mediation, but very little. One was in Natal, between UDF and Inkatha. When I was called in to mediate, the UDF said they didn't want mediation. For many reasons: one was that their leaders were in jail, another one was that they were disadvantaged and any peacemaking would institutionalise the disadvantage. If there was peacemaking and they were at the lower end, then they would remain there. So they wanted to struggle to improve their position first.
>
> So, after 10 months, it was the UDF who told me they would like to have a joint monitoring committee, because we had agreed on rules for behaviour, a code of conduct. And then they said, "without the monitoring committee, you can't control it". There's no way you can set up a joint monitoring com-mittee without meeting with the opposition. So it was at their request I then called the meeting. And they had a good meeting. So, I could say at the last, final stage I was a mediator. But for 10 months before that I was a facilitator - shuttle diplomacy.[160]

The third party — mediator, facilitator, representative, diplomat, or whatever title one uses — may be in a position to serve a variety of functions, as the situation and the protagonists change. It is not important that one always act as mediator, or that people agree on what they call different roles. What is important is the ability to dis-cern what would be useful at each moment, and try to make that possible.

In favouring a strategy of talking, one is also assuming that the talks can be pro-ductive, that settlement is possible. As John Burton describes this: "The belief, shared by the mediators, was that if only parties would interact with some degree of good faith and mutual confidence, there could be agreement."[161] It is important that these assump-tions should be examined carefully, with respect both to mediation as a general process, and in each unique situation. Burton mentions two difficulties with this assumption:

> First, there are issues on which there cannot be compromise, and second, with all the good will in the world, there may not be within the conceptual frame-work of anyone involved in such a conflict any options outside those that have been within their experience or knowledge. They might desperately desire and seek an agreement, but there is nothing within their conceptual frame-works that meets their needs.[162]

In addition to these, there are problems such as internal factionalism, external pressures from larger powers, and reluctant constituencies. Are the parties able, or could they become able, to negotiate a settlement that their side would accept? Are resources a critical issue, and are they equitably divisible? Even given good faith, leaders can only go as far as their followers will go, and followers will only push for acceptance of settlements that actually meet fundamental needs. Bringing people to the table is not enough. And choosing to spend one's time and energy, and theirs, in bringing them to the table, is only a good strategy when there is some reasonable likelihood of success.

Imbalance

Realistically, there are situations in which one side so over-powers the other that negotiations are either unlikely or unfair. A group which is much larger, stronger, and/or more powerful than the other will feel little need to compromise or meet the other's needs, even if it does somehow agree to negotiate in the first place. The smaller or weaker group may have to find other leverage, or work to change the overall situation, rather than putting its hopes in immediate talks. If the stronger group exercises its power repressively, the oppressed may be able to use moral suasion, either to change the oppressor, or to gain allies to exert pressure.

There are such situations, where most Friends' sympathies and sense of right may be with one side. In a case where the government is severely oppressing the people in that country, it may seem best for Quakers to try to bring pressure on this government to change its behaviour. Friends may express support for a "liberation" movement that is trying to overthrow this government, as many Friends did in the case of the ANC in South Africa. If the liberation movement is engaged in an "armed struggle", as the ANC was, is there a danger here of diluting our commitment to nonviolence? Can we support justice and equality without siding with the armed struggle? Conversely, can we support a long and doubtful process of mediation, when each day brings killings, blighted lives, and great suffering to many people? There have been some Friends who have continued to try to facilitate communication between the government and the ANC in a mediating type of role. At the same time, other Quakers and Quaker organisations were supporting various forms of sanctions against South Africa. And, simultaneously, Friends also supported various forms of empowerment, working to assist local people in becoming stronger, more articulate, better organised. There were times when these activities seemed to conflict with each other, but, in retrospect, it might be said that all three forms of intervention were helpful in moving the situation to the point of formal negotiations between the government and the ANC.

Neither response was necessarily wrong, but they did imply different assumptions. For those who chose to mediate or facilitate communication, the assumption was that the warring parties needed to hear each other's viewpoint and move toward some kind of direct dialogue in order to bring an end to the violence and suffering, and agree some new form of government that would be more just and inclusive of all the people of South Africa. For those who chose to support sanctions, the assumption was that the government would only be changed through forces and pressures that isolated them internationally and made life very difficult for them. Those favouring empowerment assumed that change would be brought about internally, by ordinary people, when they were able to take more control of their own lives. Is it possible that these differing assumptions and the resulting activities were somehow complementary? Would the situation have changed so dramatically in recent years if one of these forms of intervention had not happened? Perhaps not.

Different kinds of mediators

Another situation where Friends have not always agreed on the best form of intervention is the Middle East. For many years there has been Quaker involvement in work to assist the Palestinians, who have been displaced and disempowered by the Arab-Israeli conflict. There has been assistance of various kinds — nurseries in Gaza, legal aid in Jerusalem and the West Bank, Friends School in Ramallah, Brummana School in Lebanon. Quaker Peace & Service has a Middle East Placement Programme through which they place volunteers with both Israeli and Arab organisations. At another level, Quaker representatives have organised and funded conferences on various topics that have brought together diplomats, academics and others from the differing sides. There have been documents drafted by Quaker working groups that have been circulated in numerous drafts among the leading parties on each side for comment and discussion, and then published for more general circulation. Behind the scenes, there have been Friends involved in carrying of messages and arranging meetings in a mediating role.

Quakers and Quaker organisations outside the Middle East have lobbied their own governments to bring pressure on the situation in various ways. These outside governments, as well as the United Nations, have engaged in a kind of mediating role that has some pressure and influence behind it — i.e. they can threaten to withhold aid or impose sanctions if the parties don't cooperate with the process of mediation and negotiation. Sydney Bailey refers to two types of mediation:

> Weaponless mediation and mediation-with-muscle have distinct but complementary roles. If the Middle East is any guide, the main role of the weaponless mediator is to identify and clarify issues, remove misperceptions, convey information and ideas, and promote goodwill to negotiate.[163]

So the decision to become a "weaponless mediator" might be related to the possibility of filling a useful role in the particular situation. A variety of activities may be necessary, the emphasis may change over time, but the constant is the willingness to make an apparent disadvantage into an advantage.

It is also likely that different stages and different situations may call for different kinds of mediation. Clearly, there is a role for high-level, visible, "muscled" mediation by the United Nations, for example. In other situations, a regional organisation such as the Organisation for African Unity, or a sympathetic neighbour such as Haile Selassie in the 1972 Sudan negotiations,[164] may have a role to play. One-off workshops and conferences may be very helpful at certain stages, in providing opportunities for people to establish the protocols of having met, or enabling them to meet without publicity, or even just allowing individuals to seek each other out over coffee or meals.

Similarly, there will be stages when the kind of mediation described here, by invisible Quaker representatives, will have a role to play.

It is very difficult to mediate in a conflict where one of the parties feels it is able to gain its objectives through the use of force. Conflicts between parties of widely differing power are unlikely to be ready for mediation. It may be an unpalatable choice, but there are cases in which we must wait until options of violence are exhausted. People may be forced to the negotiating table, but not by NGOs.

There are, however, conflicts where all parties recognize that no side can gain a military victory.

It is often the case - perhaps it is in the very nature of violent conflict - that lines of communication between the parties have broken down. Each one is extremely hesitant to take the first step toward the other, afraid that such an approach will be interpreted as a sign of weakness. At such moments, an NGO may play a role in opening up lines of communication between the parties.

Often, in fact, governments prefer that an NGO, rather than an inter-governmental organization such as the UN, play such a role, since they would like to prevent what they see as the internationalization of the conflict.

Moreover, in a society which has become intensely polarized and in which mistrust is widespread, such a first initiative may require outsiders.[165]

Including the excluded

The ability to be in direct contact with illegal and unrecognised groups is an asset that Quaker mediators have brought to a number of conflict situations. In Northern Ireland, in the Middle East, in Sri Lanka, and in a number of other places, Quaker representatives have been able to talk with members of illegal groups and the political parties associated with them. Such intermediaries could then bring these views into discussions with members of other political organisations and governments, who were not willing to have direct talks. And the intermediaries continued to suggest that the contact should be direct, that these marginalised groups had views that needed to be heard.

But perhaps the greatest asset of the non-official weaponless mediator is the possibility of dealing with non-recognized entities. Throughout much of the Arab-Israeli conflict, the Arabs were unwilling to deal directly with Israel, and various UN, national, and non-official representatives have acted as intermediaries. But from 1964-88, there was a widespread official reluctance to deal with the Palestinian Liberation Organization until it had renounced terrorism, recognized Israel, and accepted Security Council Resolutions 242 and 338.[166]

Again, there are assumptions underlying this choice, which may have an effect on the possible outcome. Some would say that the fact of talking with people from armed or illegal groups lends them credibility that they wouldn't otherwise have. Yet the mediator is making the assumption that the violence will not end unless those who are engaged in violence can be brought into the process somehow. Governments might insist that they can defeat the armed group militarily, and that it is better to isolate these people politically. But, in this case, the government is choosing the use of violence to counter the violence being used against them. This choice may feed the spiral of escalating violence and polarisation, if illegal groups who are unable to communicate directly with politicians, use violence as a form of communication.[167] Governments are also choosing, in declaring a group illegal, to forbid the expression of a view, either because of the nature of the view (e.g., that it favours overthrowing the government) or because of the means of its expression (by force of arms). This often results in marginalising people who share some of the views of the illegal group, without necessarily favouring armed insurrection. Thus, the proscription of an organisation polarises the situation, increasing the number of people who feel their views are not heard, and making it more difficult for opponents to learn of each other's life experiences. It is this polarisation that the mediator tries to overcome.

Quaker values

In choosing to engage in mediation, Friends may have to decide that the possibility of being useful in promoting peace is more important than asserting our values and principles in a public way. But the process of mediation does not preclude the possibility of stating our values and the basis of our activity to the parties that we are engaged with. Representatives of Friends and Friends' organisations have found that people in areas where Quakers have worked previously, often expect Friends to represent certain values:

I think that the whole question of political mediation is not one that has been defined as a primary goal for this region and for our work in this region as QIAR's.[168] Donna and I sometimes talk with each other in trying to pinpoint what is our primary role here. I think that one of the things that we have come to see it as is being representative of values that the American Friends Service Committee and Quakers stand for in terms of peace and social justice and human rights and so forth. Being representatives of that organisational embodiment of those values in the region of southeast Asia and China. The reason that we've come to see that as important is that we have learned in the three years we've been here travelling around that other people see Quakers and/or the American Friends Service Committee, but particularly Quakers, as standing for this, rightly or wrongly. And therefore, by our travelling around and letting people know that we're here and who we are and so forth, several times when they have felt that there was something that needed mediation, reconciliation - I'll use these words loosely - but when they have needed someone to fill a role, they have come looking for us, because it seemed to them that we would be neutral, that we would support their cause.[169]

But do those who don't share our values find them threatening to their own system of values? For example, when Friends get involved in a country such as Sri Lanka, are we imposing a western and Christian value system on a situation where most people are eastern and either Buddhist, Hindu, or Muslim? Does this mean that the process of mediation that we might offer is actually inappropriate, or even incompatible, with what people in that situation believe? Would it be better, perhaps, to share our experience of mediation with potential mediators in that situation and empower them to become the mediators? Part of the QPS programme in Sri Lanka has been to train local people in conflict resolution skills with an expectation that they might become the peacemakers in their own country. This approach is based on an assumption that they are the ones who know their own situation best, and can therefore know best how to intervene.

On the other hand, in the case where Quakers went to Uganda to assist with mediation, they found that a number of Ugandans had got together and devised a process of mediation that looked very much like the process that the outside mediators had been using elsewhere. Many aspects of the political process were very different in Uganda than in Northern Ireland, for example: patterns of authority, decision-making, elections, the role of the military, the importance of traditional leaders. But the process of consulting people, getting opponents to communicate and then meet directly, and assisting local people to define the problems and invent ways of solving them, all seemed somehow similar in the two situations.

No single, imported model or process seems to work in another situation, but things that do work have clear similarities in process, if not in content. It may be that there are some basic elements of the mediation process that are transferable and adaptable to whatever cultural situation. These might include: willingness to listen to all sides without taking sides; the possibility of building relationships of trust with significant individuals on all sides; being able to move back and forth between these individuals without much publicity; and a commitment to stay with the process as long as necessary, but then to withdraw and get out of the way when a mediator is no longer needed.

CHAPTER 16

Universality of the Process

IN AOTEAROA/NEW ZEALAND, THE MAORI have a phrase that appears often in public discourse: "tanga te whenua", the people of the land. This phrase conveys the sense that there is something distinctive about each people, not only because of their culture, but because of their relationship to their place. Each people in each place is unique. Anyone who comes into an area wanting to do something there must first consult the "tanga te whenua", who know best what may be done there.

It should be no surprise that ways of working on conflict cannot simply be developed in one place and superimposed on another. No single imported model or process seems to work in another situation, but things that do work have clear similarities in process, if not in content. Yet, all peoples are related. Travelling to vastly different places, looking at ways of working on conflict, one finds some resonances, some familiar themes, as well as new ideas. There are people doing what we would call mediation, whether they use that term or not.

Alternatives

The crucial similarity in the different processes that constitute mediation is the possibility of an alternative. Adversaries are trapped in war, in violent political conflict of all sorts, and they can envisage no outcomes except military victory or defeat. Because people do not see the possibility of working on conflicts, they feel, as one Ugandan said, that "Peace will be possible only when we are all the same." Hence, chilling strategies like "peace walls" to separate groups and "ethnic cleansing" to ensure that only one side is left in possession of the region. The novelty of mediation is to hold out the hope of working on one's own conflict with forces other than lethal weapons, of confronting the enemy without anyone being killed, and perhaps of creating a way to live together without being the same.

Quaker mediators have not generally been responsible for the final solution of a conflict. Their role has been to offer the hope that something other than military victory and the subjugation of losers by winners may be possible. There is a search for alternative solutions, as well as the use of an alternative process: mediation itself. One Quaker mediator says that "what we are trying to do is to find something creative - getting over a problem that each one is stating."[170] The parties involved may see this problem as irreconcilable, because they state it in terms that are mutually exclusive. With the help of mediation, they are sometimes able to restate the problem and identify their needs in such a way that an alternative can be identified that would meet at least the most vital needs of all sides.

Although there may be recurring themes, the specific needs of the parties seem to vary enormously: land, identity, security, the right to culture and religion. One common element in the various situations is the right of each party to define its own needs and decide when they are met, as well as the joint decision to work toward meeting all parties' most fundamental needs, understanding that anything less is an interim measure.

The mediation process offers an alternative to continued killing, even while the killing continues. No single, imported model would do this. If the mediator arrived with a diploma and a fixed, seven-step negotiating process, the opponents would be unable to enter at stage one: sit at the same table and listen to each other. What is transferable into many cultures is the willingness to work with politicians and paramilitaries, one at a time, to create an acceptable way for them to move toward direct talks about their specific situation. The value to them lies in being able to test the waters in their own way, slowly, without public commitment, so that they can stop or change at any time, and can continue to pursue other strategies until they decide whether formal mediation is the proper next step. Although the mediator works toward a cease-fire, a final cessation of hostilities, and the eventual transformation of the political structures and even of rhetoric, she does not require these changes <u>before</u> she will help in exploring possibilities. Such prerequisites may need to be met before public talks can begin, but the quiet, unofficial process can help to move toward that point.

Working on conflict in one's own place

In travelling to a number of different countries, the authors have met many people who are trying to work on conflicts in their own situations. These people are part of the "tanga te whenua," and they understand in a profound way the past and the possible futures of their own people and their own place. Whatever impartiality outsiders may bring, it must be joined with local knowledge before it can become useful. Only those who have lived with a particular conflict for years, or possibly generations, can really understand the complexity of those people and that place.

For the most part, Quakers have intervened in conflicts outside their own homelands. They have come offering the impartiality of outsiders, and they have tried to study the local situation, but is that good enough? In Northern Ireland and South Africa, some of the Quakers acting as representatives and mediators were local people. One member of the Quaker team working on Sri Lanka is from one of the ethnic groups involved in the conflict. In the Uganda case cited in chapter 12, the outsiders acted largely as consultants, working alongside local people who continued as mediators. In Quaker work in the Middle East, outsiders have either lived in the region for several years, or have returned for frequent visits over a period of many years. But there is always the question posed by an African-American at a seminar in New York, to the authors, American Quaker mediators working elsewhere: "If you are serious about working on conflict, why aren't you living here with us, where the really hard problems are?" And there is profound truth in this. If we are serious, we live where the conflict is. And, if we are serious, we see the conflicts where we live.

<u>The universal, and the new</u>

The authors have seen in a number of conflict situations the invention of processes that are similar, yet distinctive, to meet the particular local needs. A clergyman in Fiji described how he and other church leaders had carried out a process of message-carrying which led to direct meetings between leaders of opposing sides. A previous mediation attempt by another organisation had been wrecked because of publicity, so they were very careful about confidentiality. A political leader on one of the sides did later claim credit for this mediation, but the church leaders still did not reveal their role in the process.[171]

In Mozambique, church leaders made contact with Renamo and the Frelimo government, and encouraged the sides to consider direct negotiations in order to stop the fighting and bring an end to the suffering of the people. These mediators carried a 10-point proposal in writing from the government to Renamo, but refused to explain or interpret the written message because they did not want to be perceived to be working for one side. "We have our own message for you; explaining the other's side's viewpoint is not our job," they said.[172] This refusal is not a common element in mediation, but it seemed to them to be necessary in their situation.

A South African described how he and colleagues had analysed the conflict in a particular community that was suffering from serious political tension and violence. They then spent some months building relationships of trust with people in various political groupings. The men acting as mediators, then invited members of all these groups to attend an off-the-record meeting together on a particular day. The mediators were the facilitators of the meeting and they established some ground rules at the beginning, including that each group would have equal time to speak and that no one could leave the building until the meeting had ended.[173] This was quite an interesting variant on more common ways of providing security and confidentiality for participants in a meeting. Usually, attention is devoted to inviting few, carefully selected participants, and ensuring that they say nothing publicly about what happened. In this South African case, the guest list was large and flexible, but all who came had to stay until the end, so that none could arrange for those present to be attacked, and so that all would decide together about a public statement, if any.

In Canberra, Australia, the Conflict Resolution Service handles mediation involving recent immigrants who do not speak English. Their experience was that the translators took sides, and translated so as to favour one side or bring pressure on the other. So interpreters are now trained in mediation skills, and therefore are able to see the need to be more "neutral" in the way that they interpret what is being said. This service has also found that the mediation team that works best for conflicts involving immigrants includes one mediator who is clearly an immigrant, but not from the same ethnic group as the participants in the conflict.[174]

In Perth, another group involved in mediation has been training mediators in the aboriginal community. So far, these mediation teams are working only within the aboriginal community, not yet on conflicts between the two cultures, but there is the expectation that mixed teams of mediators will be formed. Again, the experience was that it is important to have aboriginal mediators for conflicts within that community, but they mustn't belong to the particular groups involved in the dispute.[175]

In all of these ways, with minor differences and major similarities, people in different cultural and political settings work on their own conflicts. What they create reflects their particular experience, but also some elements which are universal.

Familiar themes and roles

Many of the roles of a mediator seem to be applicable in different cultures. When the authors visited a remote village in Uganda, they found someone doing work very similar to their own.

> After describing briefly how we had worked in various situations, we asked local people what needed to happen in their situation. [A sub-county chief] described his own experience at what he would not previously have called mediation.
>
> The people in his area had suffered (as ordinary people always do) in the war between rebels and soldiers. He quoted a familiar Ugandan proverb: "When elephants fight, it is the grass that is crushed." He had therefore decided that someone must get the army and rebels to call a truce, and he had himself made contacts and carried messages until a truce was arranged.
>
> This was a dangerous enterprise; indeed, he had not previously admitted publicly to his role, which we quickly supported as necessary and courageous. But we also felt the shock of the familiar, in listening to his description of what he had done, and felt that mediation must have some validity, if people in such different situations invent such similar ways to deal with conflicts.[176]

The sub-chief had never heard of mediation before, but he recognised it immediately, and knew that this was what he had been engaged in. Some of the elements that resonated when he described his activities were:

1. The individual chose to intervene because of a "concern".
2. He analysed the conflict, which led him to
3. decide who the sides were, and in what order to contact them, and
4. to identify others who could help as intermediaries, and join him in a team.
5. He expected from the beginning that everything would have to be done with complete confidentiality.
6. He established his own credibility.
7. He built relationships with and listened carefully to leaders on each side.
8. Then, he carried perceptions between the sides, and

9. brought the suffering of ordinary people to their attention, until it became possible to
10. carry messages between them and
11. arrange direct meetings.
12. He helped them to negotiate a settlement, and
13. worked with others to monitor it.
14. He ensured that each new commander who entered the area knew of this local peace treaty and respected it.
15. He claimed no credit for the settlement.

As this case shows, there are aspects of the mediation process that seem to be so familiar as to be universal. Clearly, formal training and credentials are not essential. They may be helpful, and there may be kinds of further training and support that would be useful to amateur mediators. But the reality is that most mediation, even political mediation, is done by people who live in the area, who select themselves or are selected by the opponents because of their knowledge of and concern for the local problems, and whose expertise is about the local situation rather than the theory or models of mediation. They create a process for dealing with their particular situation, and these different processes in different places resemble each other in significant ways.

Recurring processes

Everywhere, it seems, people rediscover the notion that disputants need help to work out their conflicts. One common answer is judges, who are impartial, and make the decision about who was right or wrong, and what to do next. But judges only work when both (all) sides are prepared to, or can be compelled to, put their case and accept the judge's authority over them, or are subject to some enforcement authority.

On all levels, whether family, neighbourhood, workplace, or the international scene, solutions work best if the disputants not only agree, but invent the solutions themselves. So, on all levels, lateral thinkers appear who put themselves in the middle to try to help disputants work on their own conflict in order to resolve it well. Rather than acting as judges, these mediators act as enablers.

Many of the elements identified in the story of the sub-county chief are common to other settings. There is always, at least implicitly, an analysis of the conflict and a "mapping" that shows up possible entry points or people who might bridge the divide. Thus, Fijian and Sri Lankan mediators turned to trade union leaders, South Africans to youth groups, and Quaker Middle East representatives to journalists, as politically influential groups who could meet together and with politicians. The particular group which seems especially appropriate varies with the situation, but the search for such a group, to build an alternative to stalemate, is common to the mediation processes.

There is, in so many situations, the need for someone to hold the middle ground, to communicate with and between the sides. This person must be acceptable, and must be committed. In addition, patterns around the world suggest that the mediator must also have other characteristics in order to fill the middle role.

Universal characteristics of mediators?

Like the chief, others who intervene often look for teammates or colleagues with contacts which can complement the mediator's own circle of acquaintances. In both Uganda and Mozambique, a bishop sought his counterpart from another Christian church, to give his initiative a religious but not a denominational character, because the individual churches are perceived to be linked to political groupings. In some situations, academics are sought as intermediaries or as co-mediators, because they move freely within the society, and they are seen (rather as religious people are seen) as appealing to transcendent values: knowledge, in the one case, and spiritual truth, in the other. Politicians caught up in short-term strategy and war do not necessarily want similarly hard-headed mediators. Instead, what appeals to them is an independent-mindedness and a commitment to values and the long-term good of humanity, evidenced by the mediator's willingness to share risks without immediate prospect of reward.

One universal characteristic of mediators seems to be the ability to see and make connections. They sense that two people might have something to say to each other, that one situation may hold lessons for another, or that now is the time to mention this idea to that person. But they are characteristically flexible about this, offering a suggestion tentatively, but quick to give it up or move beyond it. Their minds are not fixed on final solutions, but on processes and next steps. So the Quaker team in Rhodesia/Zimbabwe could work out arrangements for several different meetings, and not be disappointed that none of them happened. And so also a Sri Lankan mediator could make contact with several opposition figures, none of whom picked up his original idea, but one of whom suggested another possibility and proceeded with it in a different way some years later. The mediator sees and responds to the interlocutor's ideas and perceptions, rather than insisting on her own. There is, again, a special combination of arrogance and humility, in thinking that one might be able to invent something that would help solve conflicts, while being willing to offer it as a stepping-stone.

A similar detachment and flexibility are found in this kind of mediator's attitude toward her own role. This unofficial mediator is generally focused on arranging meetings that bring opponents together, and getting out of the way so that they can form their own relationship. A South African mediator who is quite vocal when he meets with one side at a time, says almost nothing when he gets two adversaries to talk together in his presence. A Ugandan intermediary brings two people together, and is content that they continue to meet, without including him or informing him. These mediators manifest a willingness to be self-effacing, and to work themselves out of a job. And these seem to be characteristics not of the particular culture, not of the "tanga te whenua", but of the individual mediators.

Unofficial mediators know that all they can do is to offer possibilities. It is for someone else to decide whether and in what form to take up those possibilities. And so the process comes full circle. We began by saying that the mediator stays in the middle by being always at the edge. In this sense as well, the mediator maintains a useful role in the middle, by being willing to be left outside the inner circle. Having moved to the middle in order to build relationships, processes, and connections, the mediator then moves willingly to the edge, to allow the participants to come together.

APPENDIX I

Definitions

THERE ARE A VARIETY OF RELATED activities — mediation, negotiation, reconciliation, conflict resolution — whose boundaries may not be entirely clear. It may be helpful to explore these a bit further in order to have a sense of whether the various activities described here fall primarily into one category or another, or several at different moments. In general, the framework used in this book is of work done in conflict situations by a third party — not necessarily an outsider, but someone not associated with any of the groups in conflict. Of course, the terms may be used in other ways, but what follows is their intended meanings in this context. They are listed more or less in order of increasing generality; in some sense, succeeding terms may include previous ones.

Contact work, which is not often used here, describes a category of reconciliation initiatives based on the assumption that the mere bringing together of opponents will change them and, therefore, the situation. The overall experience of Quakers and others is that this assumption is false, and that much more is required to promote change.

Conferences is used as a generic term, to cover a range of activities frequently associated with the work of Quaker offices and representatives. These include the arranging of meetings between scholars, technical experts, government representatives, diplomats, politicians, civil servants, leaders or spokespeople of groupings, and persons more loosely associated with particular points of view. The meetings arranged may vary in size, degree of formality, scope, and intention. Some are specific in focus, others very general so that participants may include or exclude issues at their own discretion. Some are part of a series, to which whole categories of people may be invited, such as all diplomats accredited to a particular capital. Others are one-off[177] meetings, with a carefully selected list of invitees. Most conferences have two main motivations, in some combination: to help opponents get to know each other better, and to move forward the discussion of particular issues.

The term **meetings** is generally used to refer to smaller gatherings than conferences, often with only three or four people present, and generally less formal. Often, the third party has had a part in arranging the meeting and, in many cases, may be present at the meeting. This is not an occasion when negotiation is happening, but may be an opportunity to exchange ideas about the possibility of negotiation. Often it may a getting-acquainted session.

By **facilitation** we mean the work of a third party to enable parties in conflict to meet or communicate with each other. This term often applies to a chairperson who lacks a traditional position of power or leadership, who is acceptable to all the parties, and who is focused on the process more than the outcome. It can be quite a technical role, but, because it provides a crucial link, can become much broader and quite significant. Facilitation often focuses on issues of communication, misperception, and misunderstanding. It may be limited to one event, or it can be long-term and related to a series of contacts or an on-going channel between or among sides to a conflict.

Mediation in this context refers to attempts by third parties to assist opponents in working on their shared conflict. The term **conciliation** has a similar meaning here. In its use to describe work on neighbourhood, family, and personal disputes, mediation often is taken to mean a particular process, with steps more or less as follows:

Introductions;
Each side tells its story, describes the situation;
Clarification and feelings;
Identification of issues;
Generating alternatives for solution;
Writing an agreement.

In the political realm, a negotiation process might look something like this, though generally much more formal, public, and adversarial. Much of what we describe as **political mediation** occurs before negotiations are possible, or when they break down. It often involves going through many of these steps less rigorously, with one side at a time (often called **shuttle mediation**) until or unless opponents are willing to meet directly. Our own sense is that we often take individual politicians through this mediation process separately, allowing them to try it out in safety and confidentiality, before attempting it with the opponent. Sometimes, the agreement we work toward together is simply an agreement between the two opponents to meet, with an agenda set by the identification of issues and alternatives.

We have concentrated here on political mediation to try to describe what we see as a distinct category of work. Some might use the expression **"good offices"** for many of the activities described here, in which a third party serves as an intermediary. We prefer to call this political mediation or shuttle mediation.

Negotiation is the formal, face-to-face meeting of opponents to argue their cause and reach a settlement of the conflict. It may include a third party, or not. It implies the participation of persons authorised to speak for each side, able to make an agreement on their behalf.

Reconciliation work we take to mean the long-term effort to build or rebuild relationships between people. This is aimed at the profound change from enmity, hostility, or complete separation to mutual understanding or harmonious cooperation. Because it is very long-term, many of its activities must be appreciated as steps on the way, without any expectation of immediate result. In some ways, reconciliation is the umbrella term that includes all the others.

Is this mediation?

Quaker experience in engaging in political mediation has not been as third parties in formal, public negotiations between governments or armies. It seems to us, however, that the term need not be too restrictive. In recent years, mediation has come to convey not just a process, but an approach. It is characterised by the insistence that parties to a dispute should be the ones to settle it (in preference to judges or referees, for example), and that they must decide what constitutes an acceptable settlement. The role of the third party is not to devise or enforce the solution, but to introduce or facilitate a process of joint work by the opponents on the problem they have in common. Some of the issues have to do with communication: stereotypes, polarisation, anger, mistrust. Some have to do with concrete issues: the distribution of resources, the placement of borders, the voting method, the relations between regions. In our sense, political mediation includes all of this, and more.

This is a long-term process. It involves the building of relationships, the development of ways of communicating honestly with each other, the moderation of prevailing hostility and polarisation to permit eventual joint meetings. Often, Quakers have been involved in a variety of activities intended to enable direct negotiations to occur. Sometimes the mediator has the sense of taking the participants through the mediation process, but doing it with one at a time, in the form of shuttle mediation. This may be a necessary step, to build familiarity with and trust in the process so that face-to-face discussions can occur. In these senses, we believe the work described here to fit into the broad category of political mediation.

People Interviewed and Quoted

Donna Anderton and Barbara Bird have been Quaker International Affairs Representatives of the American Friends Service Committee since 1989, first based in Hong Kong and now in Bangkok, Thailand. Donna's background is in education and consultancy. Barbara's background is in social work, community organisation, and family therapy.

Sydney Bailey is a freelance writer and consultant in London. He spent four years as a Quaker representative at the United Nations Headquarters before becoming a Visiting Research Scholar with the Carnegie Endowment for International Peace in New York. He was later a member of the British Foreign Office Advisory Committees on the United Nations and Disarmament. He has written many books about the political functions of the United Nations, and others on themes of peace and human rights. His involvement in political mediation has included the Middle East and Northern Ireland.

Adam Curle has for over 25 years been actively involved in efforts to mediate violent conflicts, in India and Pakistan, Nigeria, Rhodesia/Zimbabwe, Northern Ireland, and Sri Lanka, mostly under Quaker auspices. He was educated at Oxford University in anthropology, and has held chairs at Exeter, Ghana, Harvard and Bradford Universities in psychology, education, development and peace studies. He is the author of several books on the themes of conflict resolution, mediation, peace, and justice.

Joseph Elder is Professor of Sociology and South Asian studies at the University of Wisconsin. He has participated in Quaker mediation teams over many years, including an India-Pakistan "mission" in the mid-1960's and more recently in Sri Lanka.

Anne and J. Brewster Grace were Quaker International Affairs Representatives in the Middle East from 1988 to 1992. Based in Amman, Jordan, they made frequent visits to Israel, the West Bank and Gaza, and regularly visited Egypt and Syria. They organised a number of off-the-record meetings related to the peace process in the region. Brewster Grace is currently Representative at the Quaker United Nations Office, Geneva.

Joel McClellan is currently based in Hanoi as the representative for Church World Service. From 1984 to 1992 he was the Representative at the Quaker United Nations Office in Geneva and in that capacity was actively involved in Quaker international mediation work.

John McConnell and Erica Cadbury were Representatives of Quaker Peace & Service (QPS) in Sri Lanka from 1986 to 1989. John had previously been Education Advisor to QPS from 1982 to 1986. He has been involved in initiatives in political mediation in Sri Lanka and Burma and has led courses in mediation in India, Bangladesh, Thailand and Cambodia. While holding Visiting Fellowships at the University of Bradford (U.K.), John and Erica are currently based in Chiang Mai, Thailand, where they are writing and teaching about mediation.

Everett Mendelsohn is Professor of the History of Science at Harvard University. He has for many years been involved in visits and mediation initiatives in the former Soviet Union and in the Middle East, many of these under Quaker auspices.

N. Ramamurthy, known to colleagues and friends as "Ram", has been the Asia Secretary of Quaker Peace & Service based in London since 1983. In that capacity, he has been involved with work and contacts in many parts of Asia, with a particular focus on the Indian sub-continent. Ram spent his early life in Burma and moved to India in 1942. He is a qualified engineer with 9 years experience as a marine engineer and 25 years in the tyre industry, including several years in Ghana.

Hendrik W van der Merwe, known as HW, is a South African Quaker. He has a PhD in Sociology from the University of California. From 1968 to 1992, he was the director of the Centre for Intergroup Studies based at the University of Cape Town. The major thrust of his work has been the promotion of communication between conflicting groups in South Africa. He has written and lectured widely on issues of conflict and peace.

Sue and Steven Williams, the authors of this book, are American Quakers. As representatives of Quaker Peace & Service, they have lived and worked in Uganda (1984-86) and Northern Ireland (1987-91). They have also worked in a refugee centre in Botswana and with street children in Haiti. Steve was a teacher of science and social studies in Ethiopia, and studied at the University of Sierra Leone.

OTHER PERSONS CONSULTED

Mordechai and Erela Bar-on, Jerusalem
Alan Campbell, Perth
Kevin Clements, Christchurch, Aotearoa/New Zealand

Albert Dayile, Cape Town
Nirmalan Dhas, Colombo, Sri Lanka
Phil Esmonde and Penny Robbins, Colombo
Topsy Evans, Hobart, Tasmania, Australia
Ron and Pam Ferguson, Kampala, Uganda
Val Ferguson, London
Simon Fisher, Birmingham, England
Niall and Mari Fitzduff, Belfast
David and Beryl Gowty, Bangkok
A. Paul Hare, Israel
Tim Harris, Jerusalem
Peter Herby, Cambridge, England, and Geneva
Hizkias Assefa and Harold Miller, Nairobi
Pat Hunt, Pennsylvania, USA
David James and Jillian Wychel, Wanganui, Aotearoa/New Zealand
Corinne Johnson, Philadelphia
Tim Johnstone, Canberra
Mary Khass, Gaza
Ron Kraybill, Cape Town
Anita Kromberg and Richard Steele, Durban
Jonathan Kuttab, Jerusalem
Khalil Mahshi, West Bank
Zablon Malenge, Nairobi
Jim Matlack, Washington
Duduzile Mtshazo, Soweto, Johannesburg
Cindy Mullet, Maputo, Mozambique
Fiona McKay, Jerusalem
Rev. Paula Niukula, Lautoka, Fiji
Vuyi Nxasama, Natal
Jack Patterson and Cheshire Frager, New York
David Purnell, Canberra
Elizabeth Salter, Geneva
Jill Sanders, Hobart
Bishop Denis Singulane, Maputo
Ruth and Donald Thomas, Nairobi
Ubima p'Udongi, Kampala
Wafutseyoh El Wambi, Kampala
Harold and Nancy Wilkinson, Canberra
Anthony Wilson, Birmingham, England

Bibliography

American Friends Service Committee, Journey Through a Wall. Philadelphia, AFSC, 1964.

American Friends Service Committee, "Reconciliation in the Post Cold War Era: Challenges to Quaker International Affairs Work." Philadelphia, AFSC, 1992.

American Friends Service Committee, Search for Peace in the Middle East. Greenwich, Connecticut, Fawcett, 1970.

Azar, Edward E., and Burton, John W. (eds.), International Conflict Resolution: Theory and Practice. Sussex, Wheatsheaf Books, 1986.

Bailey, Sydney, Four Arab-Israeli Wars and the Peace Process. London, Macmillan, 1990.

Bailey, Sydney, "A Case Study in Quaker Mediation." Friends Quarterly, v.22, no.2 (1980), pp.88-95.

Bailey, Sydney, "Non-official mediation in disputes: Reflection on the Quaker experience." International Affairs, v.61, no.2 (1985), pp.205-222.

Berman, Maureen R. and Johnson, Joseph E. (eds.), Unofficial Diplomats. New York, Columbia University Press, 1977.

Blackburne, Laura D., "The Role of the Mediator in Community Disputes." In "Third Party Intervention: Mediation, Facilitation and Negotiation," Occasional Paper No. 11, Cape Town, Centre for Intergroup Studies, 1985, pp.28-33.

Bolling, Landrum, "Quaker Work in the Middle East following the June 1967 war." In Berman, M. and Johnson, E. (eds.), Unofficial Diplomats, New York, Columbia University Press, 1977, pp.80-88.

Boucher, Jerry, et.al. (eds.), Ethnic Conflict: International perspectives. Newbury Park, California, Sage, 1987.

121

Brookmire, David A., and Sistrunk, Frank, "The Effects of Perceived Ability and Impartiality of Mediators and Time Pressure on Negotiation." Journal of Conflict Resolution, v.24 (1980), pp.311-327.

Buber, Martin, I and Thou. Edinburgh, T. & T. Clark, 1937.

Burton, John W., Conflict and Communication: The Use of Controlled Communication in International Relations. London, Macmillan, and New York, The Free Press, 1969.

Burton, John, Conflict: Resolution and Provention. London, Macmillan, 1990.

Curle, Adam, In the Middle: Non-Official Mediation in Violent Situations. Leamington Spa, U.K., Berg Publishers, 1986.

Curle, Adam, Making Peace. London, Tavistock, 1971.

Curle, Adam, True Justice. London, Quaker Home Service, 1981.

Deutsch, Morton, The Resolution of Conflict: Constructive and Destructive Processes. New Haven, Yale University Press, 1973.

Hare, A. Paul, Cyprus Resettlement Project: An Instance of International Peacemaking. Beer Sheva, Ben Gurion University of the Negev, 1984.

Hare, A. Paul (ed.), The Struggle for Democracy in South Africa: Conflict and Conflict Resolution. Cape Town, Centre for Intergroup Studies, 1983.

Hare, A. Paul, "Quaker Mediation in National and International Conflicts." Unpublished paper, Beer Sheva, Ben Gurion University, 1992.

Hizkias Assefa, Mediation of Civil Wars: Approaches and Strategies - The Sudan Conflict. Boulder & London, Westview Press, 1987.

Jackson, Elmore, Meeting of Minds: A Way to Peace Through Mediation. New York, McGraw-Hill, 1952.

Jackson, Elmore, Middle East Mission. New York, Norton, 1983.

Levy, Marc A., "Mediation of Prisoners' Dilemma Conflicts and the Importance of the Cooperation Threshold: the Case of Namibia." Journal of Conflict Resolution, v.29, no.4 (Dec. 1985), pp.581-603.

London Yearly Meeting of the Religious Society of Friends, Church Government. London, 1968.

McClellan, Joel, "On Mediation: An NGO Role?" In One World, No. 175, May 1992, Geneva, World Council of Churches, pp.5-7.

MacDonald, John W., jr., and Bendahmane, Diane B. (eds.), Conflict Resolution: Track Two Diplomacy. Washington, D.C., Foreign Service Institute, 1987.

Martin, Walter, "Quaker Diplomacy as Peace Witness." The Friend, v.142, no.31, August 3, 1984, p.973.

Mendelsohn, Everett, A Compassionate Peace: A Future for Israel, Palestine, and the Middle East. New York, Noonday Press, 1989. (earlier edition: New York, Hill & Wang, 1982.)

Mitchell, C.R., and Webb, K. (eds.), New Approaches to International Mediation. New York, Westport (Connecticut), and London, Greenwood Press, 1988.

Moulton, Phillips P. (ed.), The Journal and Major Essays of John Woolman. New York, Oxford University Press, 1971.

Northedge, F.S., and Donelan, M.D., International Disputes: The Political Aspects. London, Europa Publications, 1971.

Pickett, Clarence E., For More than Bread. Boston, Little, Brown & Co., 1953.

Podolefsky, Aaron, "Mediator Roles in Simbu Conflict Management." Ethnology, v.29 (1990), pp.67-81.

Quaker Peace & Service, Quaker Experience of Political Mediation. London, QPS, revised 1992. (first published in 1990)

Ross, Marc Howard, "Internal and External Conflict and Violence: Cross-Cultural Evidence." Journal of Conflict Resolution, v.29, no.4 (1985), p.547.

Stephenson, Carolyn M. (ed.), Alternative Methods for International Security. Washington, University Press of America, 1982.

Touval, Saadia, and Zartman, I. William (eds.), International Mediation in Theory and Practice. Boulder, Colorado, Westview Press, 1985.

Ullmann, Richard K., The Dilemmas of a Reconciler. London, Quaker Peace & Service, 1984.

van der Merwe, H W, Pursuing Justice and Peace in South Africa. London, Routledge, 1989.

van der Merwe, H W, "Mediation and Empowerment: Quaker Efforts Towards Peace and Justice in South Africa." Research Paper No. 4, Cape Town, Centre for Intergroup Studies, 1984.

van der Merwe, H W, "Political Facilitation and Mediation in South Africa." Paper presented at the National Workshop of the Five Freedoms Forum, Pretoria, 1-3 February 1991. Cape Town, Centre for Intergroup Studies, 1991.

van der Merwe, H W, "South Africa: Morality and Action." Unpublished lectures given at Haverford College, 17-18-19 September, 1980.

van der Merwe, H W, and Williams, Sue K., "Pressure and cooperation as complimentary aspects of the process of communication between conflicting parties in South Africa." Paradigms, v.1, no.1 (1987), pp.8-13.

Wehr, Paul, and Lederach, John Paul, "Mediating Conflict in Central America." Journal of Peace Research, v.28 (1991), pp.85-98.

Wells, Miriam J., "Mediation, Dependency, and the Goals of Development." The American Ethnologist, v.10 (1983), pp.770-788.

Williams, Steven A. and Williams, Sue K., "Reflections on Mediation." Unpublished paper, Cape Town, Centre for Intergroup Studies, 1991.

Williams, Sue K. and Williams, Steven A., "Mediation in Africa: Some observations." Unpublished paper, Belfast, QPS, 1992.

Williams, Sue K., "Innocence." The Friends' Quarterly, July, 1992.

Williams, Sue K., "On Developing Relationships in Non-Official (Quaker) Political Mediation." Unpublished paper, Belfast, QPS, 1990.

Yarrow, C. H. Mike, Quaker Experience in International Conciliation. New Haven, Yale University Press, 1978.

Young, Oran R., The Intermediaries: Third Parties in International Crisis. Princeton, New Jersey, Princeton University Press, 1967.

Zartman, I. William, and Touval, Saadia, "International Mediation: Conflict Resolution and Power Politics." The Journal of Social Issues, v.41, no.2 (1985), pp.27-45.

Index of Names and Places

Notes

1 In this document, the two terms Quaker and Friend will be used interchangeably to denote a member of the Religious Society of Friends.

2 In early 1992, Ireland Yearly Meeting decided to establish its own organisation. Henceforth, Quaker Peace & Service is and will be a department of London Yearly Meeting.

3 This consultation produced the document Quaker experience of political mediation, (Quaker Peace & Service, London, 1990.)

4 The Carter Center of Emory University in Atlanta, Georgia, USA, was started by former American President Jimmy Carter. It includes a Conflict Resolution Program and is the base for the International Negotiation Network which coordinates third-party assistance in a number of conflicts around the world.

5 London Yearly Meeting of the Religious Society of Friends, Church Government, approved 1967. London, 1968, Chapter 25, section 861.

6 Adam Curle, talk on "Peacemaking: The Middle Way" at Quaker International Affairs Colloquium, in Reconciliation in the Post Cold War Era. Philadelphia, AFSC, 1992, p. 9.

7 H W van der Merwe, "Mediation and Empowerment" in The Struggle for Democracy in South Africa: Conflict and Conflict Resolution, edited by A. Paul Hare. Capetown, Centre for Intergroup Studies, 1983, pp. 28-29.

8 C. H. Mike Yarrow, Quaker Experiences in International Conciliation. New Haven and London, Yale University Press, 1978, p.162.

9 see ibid., p.168.

10 Everett Mendelsohn, taped conversation with the authors, Boston, 24 April 1992, p.19.

11 Trevor Jepson, "Zimbabwe Case Study", in Quaker Experience of Political Mediation. London, Quaker Peace & Service, 1990, Appendix C:I, p.3.

12 Everett Mendelsohn, taped conversation, pp.17-18.

13 Walter Martin, "Quaker Diplomacy as Peace Witness", in The Friend, v.142, no.31, August 3, 1984, p. 973.

14 Clarence E. Pickett, For More Than Bread. Boston, Little, Brown and Company, 1953, p. 140.

15 Elmore Jackson, Middle East Mission. New York and London, Norton, 1983, pp. 24-25.

16 J. Brewster Grace. Talk delivered at Quaker International Affairs Colloquium held on 17 January 1992, in Reconciliation in the Post Cold War Era: Challenges to Quaker International Affairs Work. Philadelphia, AFSC, 1992, pp.12-13.

17 C.H. Mike Yarrow, Quaker Experiences in International Conciliation. New Haven and London, Yale University Press, 1978, pp. 43-47.

18 Ibid., pp. 40-43.

19 N. Ramamurthy, taped conversation with the authors, London, 3 December 1992, p.2.

20 Anne Grace, taped conversation with the authors, Amman, Jordan, 10 March 1992, p.10.

[21] Steven Williams, unpublished manuscript, Uganda, 1991.

[22] Simon Fisher, in conversation with the authors, Birmingham, England, 10 November 1992.

[23] Joel McClellan, taped conversation with the authors, Geneva, 5 March 1992, pp. 1-2.

[24] Everett Mendelsohn, taped conversation with authors, p. 1.

[25] H W van der Merwe, taped conversation with the authors, Cape Town, 19 November 1991, p.4.

[26] Steven Williams, unpublished manuscript, Belfast, 1991.

[27] Khalil Mahshi, in conversation with the authors, 31 March 1992, Ramallah, West Bank.

[28] At least one Quaker mediator views the linking of "balance" and "partiality" as confusing and possibly contradictory. "Balanced partiality", as it is used here, reflects the belief of the authors, shared by some other mediators, that one can become attached to all sides, rather than remaining detached from any side. This requires a discipline of demonstrating genuine concern for and understanding of the situation of each of the parties to the conflict. It is possible to begin from a concern for one of the sides and then to develop a similar concern for the other sides. See reference to this in relation to the India Conciliation Group in Quaker Experience of Political Mediation. London, Quaker Peace & Service, 1992, p.6.

[29] Steven and Sue Williams, "Reflections on Mediation", Cape Town, November 1991, p.2.

[30] H W van der Merwe, taped conversation with authors, 19 November 1991, p.5.

[31] Steven and Sue Williams, in panel on "Cross-cultural mediation," 4th Conference on Negotiation and Mediation in South Africa, at Peninsula Technikon, Bellville, S.A., 28 November 1991.

[32] Bishop Denis Singulane, in conversation with the authors, Maputo, 31 December 1991.

[33] Barbara Bird, taped conversation with the authors, Bangkok, 15 September 1992, p.6.

[34] As described in the Preface, the authors' intention is to refer to a mediator as "she" and to a political figure as "he" simply as a convenient way of distinguishing them in sentences.

[35] Martin Buber, I and Thou. Edinburgh, T. & T. Clark, 1937.

[36] John McConnell, taped conversation with the authors, Chiang Mai, Thailand, 14 September 1992, p.5.

[37] Sue Williams, "On Developing Relationships in Non-official (Quaker) Political Mediation". Belfast, 1990, pp.5-6.

[38] Sydney Bailey, in letter to the authors, 16/12/92.

[39] John McConnell, taped conversation with authors, pp.1-2.

[40] Joel McClellan, taped conversation with authors, p.12.

[41] John McConnell, taped conversation with authors, p. 2.

[42] N. Ramamurthy, taped conversation with authors, p.3.

[43] Steven Williams, in taped conversation with Joseph Elder, Madison, Wisconsin, 17 June 1992, p.5.

[44] Everett Mendelsohn, taped conversation with authors, p.1.

[45] Joel McClellan, taped conversation with authors, pp. 8-9.

[46] N. Ramamurthy, taped conversation with the authors, p.8.

[47] Anne Grace, taped conversation with the authors, p.8.

[48] Sue Williams, unpublished manuscript, Belfast, 1991.

[49] Steven Williams, unpublished manuscript, Belfast, 1991.

[50] Joe Elder, taped conversation with the authors, Madison, Wisconsin, 17 June 1992, p.14.

[51] Joe Elder, ibid., p.14.

52 Sue Williams, talk given at Quaker International Affairs Colloquium, 17 January 1992, in Reconciliation in the Post Cold War Era: Challenges to Quaker International Affairs Work. Philadelphia, AFSC, 1992, p.20.

53 Sydney Bailey, in a letter to the authors dated 16/12/92, offers this note of caution: "It is a Quaker instinct to want to get the parties meeting face to face, [...] but the timing and the setting have to be absolutely right. Whenever Begin and Sadat met, they made the situation worse; after one disastrous face-to-face meeting at Camp David, President Carter insisted that they negotiate with him rather than with each other."

54 Stephen Collett, at Quaker International Affairs Colloquium, 17 January 1992, in Reconciliation in the Post Cold War Era: Challenges to Quaker International Affairs Work. Philadelphia, AFSC, 1992, p.24.

55 Peter Herby, in conversation with the authors, Cambridge, England, 4 February 1992.

56 N. Ramamurthy, taped conversation with the authors, p.10.

57 Steven Williams, unpublished manuscript, Belfast, 1991.

58 Donna Anderton, taped conversation with the authors, Bangkok, 15 September 1992, p.16.

59 J. Brewster Grace, talk given at Quaker International Affairs Colloquium, 17 January 1992, in Reconciliation in the Post Cold War Era: Challenges to Quaker International Affairs Work. Philadelphia, AFSC, 1992, p.11.

60 Sue Williams, in taped conversation with Everett Mendelsohn, Boston, 24 April 1992, p.25.

61 Everett Mendelsohn, taped conversation with authors, p.1.

62 J. Brewster Grace, taped conversation with the authors, Amman, Jordan, 12 March 1992, p.32.

63 Sydney Bailey, Four Arab-Israeli Wars and the Peace Process. London, Macmillan, 1990, p.425.

64 see C.H. Mike Yarrow, Quaker Experiences in International Conciliation, op.cit.

65 see Elmore Jackson. Middle East Mission. New York and London, Norton, 1983.

66 see A. Paul Hare, editor, Cyprus Resettlement Project: An Instance of International Peacemaking. Beer Sheva, Ben Gurion University of the Negev, 1984.

67 A. Paul Hare, "Quaker Mediation in National and International Conflicts", March 1992, p. 6.

68 N. Ramamurthy, taped conversation with authors, pp.9-10.

69 American Friends Service Committee, Journey Through a Wall. Philadelphia, AFSC, 1964.

70 C.H. Mike Yarrow, op. cit., p. 86.

71 Roland Warren, "QIAR Activities in the Divided Germany 1962-1973", in Quaker Experience of Political Mediation, London, Quaker Peace & Service, 1990. Case study III, p. 13.

72 American Friends Service Committee, Search for Peace in the Middle East. Greenwich, Connecticut, Fawcett, 1970.

73 Landrum R. Bolling, "Quaker Work in the Middle East Following the June 1967 War", in Unofficial Diplomats, edited by Maureen R. Berman and Joseph E. Johnson. New York, Columbia University Press, 1977, pp. 81 & 87.

74 Pat Hunt (former Africa Secretary, American Friends Service Committee), in conversation with the authors, Moylan, Pennsylvania, 30 April 1992.

75 Everett Mendelsohn, taped conversation with authors, pp. 11-12.

76 Anne Grace, taped conversation with authors, p.27.

77 The authors' use of the concept "balanced partiality" is explained in Chapter 3, Being in the Middle.

[78] Adam Curle, talk on "Peacemaking: The Middle Way" at Quaker International Affairs Colloquium, 17 January 1992, in Reconciliation in the Post Cold War Era: Challenges to Quaker International Affairs Work. Philadelphia, AFSC, 1992, p.5.

[79] Sue Williams, "On Developing Relationships in Non-official (Quaker) Political Mediation". Belfast, December 1990, p.6.

[80] Joe Elder, taped conversation with authors, p.18.

[81] Roland Warren, Case Study: "Quaker International Affairs Representatives' activities in the divided Germany, 1962-73," in Quaker Experience of Political Mediation. London, Quaker Peace & Service, 1992. Appendix C:III, p.xxiv.

[82] Ibid., p.xxvi.

[83] N. Ramamurthy, taped conversation with authors, p.6.

[84] Ibid., p.6.

[85] Adam Curle, taped conversation with the authors, London, 7 April 1992, p.15.

[86] Joel McClellan, taped conversation with authors, p.10-11.

[87] Sue Williams, in a mediation training seminar on behalf of the Soviet Peace Committee, Moscow, June 1991.

[88] Adam Curle, talk on "Peacemaking: The Middle Way" at Quaker International Affairs Colloquium, 17 January 1992, in Reconciliation in the Post Cold War Era: Challenges to Quaker International Affairs Work. Philadelphia, AFSC, 1992, p.9. For a more detailed quotation, see chapter 12, section entitled "Unintended Results".

[89] Sue Williams, in talk at Quaker International Affairs Colloquium, 17 January 1992, in Reconciliation in the Post Cold War Era. Philadelphia, AFSC, 1992, p.20.

[90] Joe Elder, taped conversation with authors, p.9.

[91] Joel McClellan, taped conversation with authors, p.2.

[92] Quaker Peace & Service, Quaker Experience of Political Mediation. London, QPS, 1992, p.13.

[93] N. Ramamurthy, taped conversation with authors, p.3.

[94] Ibid., p.4.

[95] Kate Kemp, "Comments by Project Members" in Cyprus Resettlement Project: An Instance of International Peacemaking, ed. by A. Paul Hare. Beer Sheva, Ben Gurion University, 1984, p. 60.

[96] T.J. Pickvance, "Third Party Mediation In National Minority Disputes: Some Lessons from the South Tyrol Problem", in New Approaches to International Mediation, edited by C.R. Mitchell and K. Webb. New York, Westport (Connecticut), and London, Greenwood Press, 1988, p.136.

[97] Joel McClellan, taped conversation with authors, p.12.

[98] Steve Williams, in taped conversation with H W van der Merwe, Cape Town, 19 November 1991, p.3.

[99] Everett Mendelsohn, taped conversation with authors, p.24.

[100] Sue Williams, in taped conversation with Brewster and Anne Grace, Amman, 10 March 1992, p.3.

[101] J. Brewster Grace, taped conversation with authors, p.34.

[102] Everett Mendelsohn, taped conversation with authors, p.14.

[103] Joe Elder, taped conversation with authors, p.3.

[104] Joe Elder, op. cit., p.20.

[105] Everett Mendelsohn, taped conversation with authors, p.28.

[106] Sue and Steve Williams, "Mediation in Africa: Some observations." Belfast, QPS, 1992. (unpublished paper)

[107] Joe Elder, taped conversation with authors, p.20.

[108] Joe Elder, taped conversation with the authors, p.30.

[109] Phil Esmonde, taped conversation with the authors, Colombo, 19 September 1992, pp. 4-5.

[110] Joe Elder, taped conversation with authors, p.31.

[111] C.H. Mike Yarrow, "Unofficial Third-Party Conciliation in International Conflicts" in Alternative Methods for International Security, edited by Carolyn M. Stephenson. Washington, D.C., University Press of America, 1982, p.123.

[112] David A. Brookmire and Frank Sistrunk, "The Effects of Perceived Ability and Impartiality of Mediators and Time Pressure on Negotiation" in Journal of Conflict Resolution, v.24 (2), 1980, pp.311-327.

[113] For case studies about work between the two Germanies, in the India-Pakistan War of 1965, and in the Nigerian Civil War of 1967-70, see C.H. Mike Yarrow, Quaker Experiences in International Conciliation, New Haven and London, Yale University Press, 1978; for case studies from Zimbabwe, the Middle East, East-West Relations, South Africa, and Northern Ireland, see Quaker Experience of Political Mediation, London, Quaker Peace & Service, 1990; for a case study from South Tyrol, see T.J. Pickvance, "Third-Party Mediation in National Minority Disputes: Some Lessons from the South Tyrol Problem", in New Approaches to International Mediation, edited by C.R. Mitchell and K. Webb, New York, Westport (Connecticut) and London, Greenwood Press, 1988, pp.131-146. Other published accounts of initiatives in the Middle East by Friends include: Elmore Jackson, Middle East Mission, London and New York, Norton, 1983; Landrum Bolling, "Quaker Work in the Middle East following the June 1967 war", in M. Berman and E. Johnson (eds.), Unofficial Diplomats, New York, Columbia University Press, 1977, pp. 80-8; and Sydney D. Bailey, "A Case Study in Quaker Mediation", Friends Quarterly, vol. 26, no. 2 (1990), pp. 88-95.

[114] Sydney Bailey, taped conversation with the authors, London, 5 February 1992, p.7.

[115] Adam Curle, taped conversation with authors, p.4.

[116] H W van der Merwe, in conversations with the authors, Cape Town, January 1992.

[117] C.H. Mike Yarrow, Quaker Experiences in International Conciliation. New Haven and London, Yale University Press, 1978, p.168.

[118] Sydney Bailey, taped conversation with authors, p.7.

[119] N. Ramamurthy, taped conversation with authors, pp.2-3.

[120] see Paul Wehr and John Paul Lederach, "Mediating Conflict in Central America," in Journal of Peace Research, v.28. Oslo, Norway, February 1991, pp.85-98.

[121] Adam Curle, in submission to Quaker Peace & Service's Uganda Mediation Support Group, London, 1991.

[122] Phil Esmonde, taped conversation with authors, p.6.

[123] John McConnell, taped conversation with authors, p.3.

[124] Tim Harris, in conversation with the authors, Jerusalem, March 1992.

[125] Ron Kraybill, "Transition from Rhodesia to Zimbabwe: The Role of Religious Actors", 10 October 1992, final draft of chapter 10 of a forthcoming book entitled Religion, The Mission Dimension of Statecraft, eds. Douglas Johnston and Cynthia Sampson (scheduled for publication by Oxford University Press, late 1993/early 1994).

[126] Joe Elder, taped conversation with authors, p.1.

[127] see Quaker Peace & Service, Quaker Experience of Political Mediation. London, QPS, 1992.

[128] Joel McClellan, taped conversation with authors, p.11.

[129] Quaker Peace & Service, Quaker Experience of Political Mediation. London, QPS, 1992, p.6.

[130] Adam Curle, taped conversation with the authors, p.7.

[131] Adam Curle, talk on "Peacemaking: The Middle Way" at Quaker International Affairs Colloquium, 17 January 1992, in Reconciliation in the Post Cold War Era: Challenges to Quaker International Affairs Work. Philadelphia, AFSC, 1992, p.9.

[132] Minutes of East-West Africa Committee of Quaker Peace & Service, London.

[133] Minutes of East-West Africa Committee of QPS, London.

[134] Ibid.

[135] Donna Anderton, in taped conversation with authors, p.17.

[136] see case study by Trevor Jepson, in Quaker Experience of Political Mediation, London, Quaker Peace & Service, 1992, Appendix C-I, pp.x–xviii.

[137] Ron Kraybill, "Transition from Rhodesia to Zimbabwe: The Role of Religious Actors", 10 October 1992, final draft of chapter 10 of a forthcoming book entitled Religion, The Mission Dimension of Statecraft, eds. Douglas Johnston and Cynthia Sampson (scheduled for publication by Oxford University Press, late 1993/early 1994).

[138] see The Journal and Major Essays of John Woolman, edited by Phillips P. Moulton, New York, Oxford University Press, 1971, p.175.

[139] Mike Yarrow, op. cit., p.274.

[140] H W van der Merwe, taped conversation with the authors, Capetown, 24 November 1991, p.6.

[141] N. Ramamurthy, taped conversation with authors, p.11.

[142] Everett Mendelsohn, taped conversation with authors, p.7; Brewster and Anne Grace, taped conversation with authors, p.22.

[143] Adam Curle, taped conversation with authors, p.14; see also Sydney Bailey, taped conversation with authors, p.4.

[144] Joel McClellan, taped conversation with authors, p.3.

[145] Everett Mendelsohn, taped conversation with authors, p.18.

[146] Sydney Bailey, taped conversation with authors, p.1.

[147] Roland Warren, in Quaker Experience of Political Mediation, Quaker Peace & Service, London, 1992, p.14.

[148] Everett Mendelsohn, taped conversation with authors, p.24.

[149] J. Brewster Grace, taped conversation with authors, p.28.

[150] Anne Grace, taped conversation with authors, p.29.

[151] H W van der Merwe, taped conversation with authors, 19 November 1991, p.3.

[152] John McConnell, taped conversation with authors, p.5.

[153] Joe Elder, taped conversation with authors, p.11.

[154] C.R. Mitchell, "The Motives for Mediation", in New Approaches to International Mediation, edited by C.R. Mitchell and K. Webb. New York, Westport (Connecticut), and London, Greenwood Press, 1988, p.33.

[155] H W van der Merwe, "Political Facilitation and Mediation in South Africa," paper presented at National Workshop of the Five Freedoms Forum, Pretoria, February 1991, p. 9.

[156] William Zartman and Saadia Touval, "International Mediation: Conflict Resolution and Power Politics", in Journal of Social Issues, Vol. 41, No. 2, 1985, pp. 32,33.

[157] C.R. Mitchell, op. cit., pp.36-37.

[158] Anne Grace, taped conversation with authors, p.33.

[159] Steve and Sue Williams, "Reflections on Mediation," unpublished paper, Cape Town, 15/11/91.

[160] H W van der Merwe, taped conversation with the authors, 19 November 1991, pp.2-3.

[161] John Burton. Conflict: Resolution and prevention. London, Macmillan, 1990, p.222.

[162] John Burton, ibid.

[163] Sydney D. Bailey. Four Arab-Israeli Wars and the Peace Process. London, Macmillan, 1990, p. 424.

[164] see Hizkias Assefa. Mediation of Civil Wars: Approaches and Strategies - the Sudan Conflict. Boulder, Westview Press, 1987.

[165] Joel McClellan, "On Mediation," One World, no.175, May, 1992. Geneva, World Council of Churches, pp.6-7.

[166] Sydney Bailey, Four Arab-Israeli Wars, pp.424-5.

[167] see H W van der Merwe and Sue Williams, "Pressure and cooperation as complementary aspects of the process of communication between conflicting parties in South Africa," Paradigms 1(1):8-13, 1987.

[168] QIAR is an abbreviation of Quaker International Affairs Representatives, usually responsible for keeping up with developments in a geographic region spanning many countries, such as Southern Africa or Central America.

[169] Barbara Bird, taped conversation with authors, p.1.

[170] N. Ramamurthy, taped conversation, p.5.

[171] Rev. Paula Niukula, in conversation with the authors, Fiji, 24 June 1992.

[172] Bishop Denis Singulane, in conversation with the authors, Maputo, 31 December 1991.

[173] Abel Majola, case study on "Getting to the Table" presented at Fourth Conference on Negotiation and Mediation in Community and Political Conflict in South Africa, 28 November 1991, Bellville, South Africa.

[174] Steve and Sue Williams, "Report of Visits in Fiji, New Zealand/Aotearoa, and Australia." Unpublished paper, London, QPS, 1992, p.4.

[175] Ibid., p.6.

[176] Sue K. and Steven A. Williams, "Mediation in Africa: Some observations." Unpublished paper, Belfast, 1992, p.1.

[177] "One-off" is an expression meaning something that happens on only one occasion and is not part of a series of events.